Welcome

A Prayerful Reflection
on the Sacrament of Reconciliation
Phelim McGowan, SJ

Illustrations
Jocelyn Merivale

Services of Reconciliation
Flor McCarthy, SDB

First published (1998) by
Dominican Publications
42 Parnell Square
Dublin 1

ISBN 1-871552-68-0

British Library Cataloguing in Publications Data.
A catalogue record for this book is available
from the British Library.

Scripture quotations are taken from the Jerusalem Bible,
published and copyright 1966, 1967 and 1968
by Darton, Longman and Todd Ltd
and Doubleday and Company Inc
and used by permission of the publishers.

Cover design by David Cooke

Printed in Ireland by
Betaprint, Dublin.

Acknowledgements

I express my gratitude to all who have made the publication of this book possible; especially the parishioners of the Sacred Heart Parish, Wimbledon. In particular I wish to record my thanks to Evelyn Bleasdale for her untiring work on the computer and to Jocelyn Merivale whose artistic insights add a further dimension to my words; without their help the script would never have seen the light of day. I am indebted to the following authors for the inspiration I gained from their writings: L. Evely, E. Farrell, J. McManus, J Maloney, H. Nouwen, A. Padovano and P. Verity and many others.

Above all I am grateful to my fellow Jesuits, Fathers J. Hyde and P. Kennedy, for their deep spirituality and the influence it had on me.

Fr. Phelim McGowan S.J.
Sacred Heart
Wimbledon
October, 1996

Contents

Services of Reconciliation

Introduction

It is necessary to explain 'love of God the Father' in order to understand the Sacrament of Reconciliation. This book endeavours to do this and is, therefore, written so that we can pray it rather than just read it. For this reason, scripture is frequently quoted throughout the book and these quotes should be read aloud (not just silently) until they permeate us. This life of Jesus, the way he lives, the way he reconciles, is an expression of the Father's love for us. His way of loving us is the Good News bringing pardon and peace. This is why the approach taken to reconciliation in this book is positive.

God the Father is always instilling in us peace, sorrow and joy and we have only to lay ourselves open to this love and we will respond to him. He does this through whatever state of life we have chosen. Chapter 15, therefore, is written by parishioners, in various states of life and each culminates in a personalised, prayerful reflection of Matthew Chapter 25.

Once we have experienced the Father's constant love for us, we can understand the enormity of our rejection of him. Ultimately, the goal of this book is to enable us to become as forgiving, as the Father in the parable of "the Prodigal Son and the Dutiful Son", who is equally loving and generous to both his sons. But this is an ongoing process of maturity, which will take a lifetime to accomplish.

How can we use this book?

Firstly, the way the book is written enables us to pray as we read it and this will give us a good grasp of reconciliation in all its aspects.

Secondly, we can pray chapter 11, 'Looking at My Life: With God' and this will show us how to experience reconciliation in everyday life, especially from God's point of view. We could do this weekly; over a period of time, reconciliation will become natural to us. Alternatively, we could look at this chapter daily, taking just one stage one day, followed by the succeeding stage next day, thus completing it in five days.

Thirdly, to prepare directly for the actual sacrament, we can pray chapter 15, 'Reconciliation: Preparing for a Public Sign', taking whichever section relates to our own state of life, including the parable of 'The Last Judgement' at the end of the chapter. Preparation can be rounded off by reading the short epilogue, Chapter 16, 'Reconciliation - Celebrating the Sign.'

Chapter One
The Trinity: Model of Friendship

'God is love' (1 Jn 4:8)

Sacred Scripture tells me categorically that I am made in God's image (Gn 1:26) and that I grow to be more like him. Because God, who is love, accepts me totally as I am, not as I ought to be, this love is enabling me to grow into my true self, to become more fully me. When I feel loved, I blossom (Lk 2:52).

I will feel loved if I allow a loving friendship between God and me to grow and deepen; but just as plants and bulbs require the right conditions for growth so does friendship. God himself shows us the conditions that are needed for the loving friendship between us to flourish: privacy and solitude. We can, however, have too much of a good thing. If a plant is exposed to nothing but sunshine it dies, incessant rain would drown a

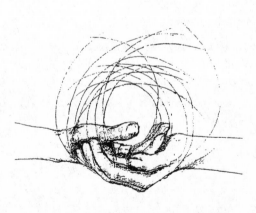

plant; but, alternative periods of sun and rain allow the plant to flourish.

Similarly, for a friendship to grow, we need space as well as togetherness. And so each of us allows ourselves the periods of solitude that we need for any friendship to grow (Ho 2:14). For the seeds of God's friendship to take root within me, I need that quiet and silence that is experienced in prayer. Like any lover, the Father speaks to me in the intimacy of quietness. But I have to wait patiently in readiness for this experience, and in complete trust in his love for me (Is 55:10-11). In their first stage of growth seeds thrive best in the dark. They grow towards the light, constantly seeking it, but too early exposure to it will limit their growth. On the other hand, if they do not find the light at all they wither and die. God loves me and knows what is best for me, so I must allow God to come to me as and when he wants. This freedom is the greatest sign of friendship I can give him. It is the gift of trust that is vital in any friendship. I need to trust as Job trusted, but it is a risk, and so I am fearful.

> 'I know that you are all powerful:
> what you conceive, you can perform.
> I am the person who obscured your designs
> with my empty-headed words.
> I have been holding forth on matters I cannot understand, on marvels
> beyond me and my knowledge.
> (Listen, I have more to say,
> now it is my turn to ask questions and yours to inform me.)
> I knew you then only by hearsay;
> but now, having seen you with my own eyes,
> I retract all that I have said,
> and in dust and ashes I repent' (Jb 42:1-6).

God the Father wants me to become my true self — and if I am to be friends with him I have to trust that through the power of his Spirit, my inner self will grow strong (Ep 3:16-19). This is not easy and I need to ask the Holy Spirit to help me trust that the Father will fashion me into his work of art (Ep 2:10).

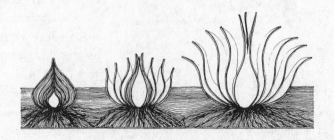

God is the divine artist

In describing God as the divine artist, Paul gives me an insight into the type of loving Father that God is. I am his work of art. No human artist, however good, is able to breathe life into his creation yet, that is what God has done for me (Gn 2:7). He has fashioned me into his own image and I can become like him (Gn 1:2).

Because the Father breathes life into me, I am able to respond to his love. I only have to accept the breath of divine life and co-operate with his touch to become like him.

> 'And we, with our unveiled faces reflecting like mirrors the brightness of the Lord, all grow brighter and brighter as we are turned into the image that we reflect; this is the work of the Lord who is Spirit' (2 Co 3:18).

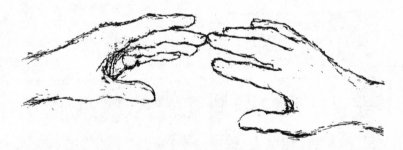

Just as the sculptor rejoices when he sees that the statue before him has realised his inspiration, so the Holy Spirit rejoices when she/he sees the divine inspirations realised in a human being. Yet no artist has ever rejoiced the way the Father rejoices over his masterpiece; his creation of 'the Word made flesh' (Jn 1:14).

Irenaeus, one of the Greek Fathers of the 2nd century, believed that 'the splendour of God is a person fully realised'. In the divine friendship God is creating me and, as I grow in his love, I am going from creation to re-creation (Jr 31:3-4).

The Holy Spirit is breath

Jesus the human person, responded totally to the breath of the divine Artist, so that in him the Holy Spirit had full sway. At the Annunciation of his birth, when Mary asked 'how can this come about?' the angel answered: 'The Holy Spirit will come upon you' (Lk 1:35).

By the time of his death Jesus had become the perfect human person, able to say 'It is accomplished', bow his head and give up his Spirit (Jn 19:30). Through him the gift of God's breath became God's gift to us all. After his Resurrection, he appeared to his disciples and said: 'As the Father sent me, so am I sending you'. Then he breathed on them and said:

'Receive the Holy Spirit. For those whose sins you forgive,
they are forgiven; for those whose sins you retain,
they are retained' (Jn 20:22).

Thus, like Jesus, we too, his disciples, may become the sons and daughters of the Father and live in loving friendship with him and with one another, but we can also do more. We are invited to join in God's work of creation and recreation. Through our experience of the love of the Father, the example of the Son, and the power of the Spirit, we learn the meaning of friendship and love; we know how to be free and how to enable each other to grow, how to reach our full potential and become mature, responsible friends in God's image and likeness.

Chapter Two
Friendship: A Father's Dream

The Father's masterpiece

I am made in God's image, but I will only realise this if I look closely at Jesus, 'a person like me in all things but sin.' Just like me, he was made in God's image but, unlike me, he always, unfailingly, responds to his Father's love with gratitude. He responds to love with love. In order to become a true son or daughter, I need to delight in my relationship with the Father.

'Everyone moved by the Spirit is the son or daughter of God. The Spirit I received is not the spirit of slaves, bringing fear....... it is the spirit of sons and daughters and it makes me cry out 'Abba Father'. The Spirit herself and our spirit bear witness that I am a child of God.' (Rm 8:14-16).

I will only become a true image of the Father when I have acquired the

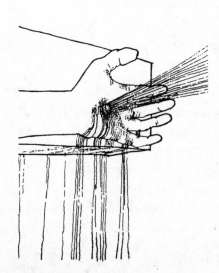

mind of Jesus (Ph 2:5) and am filled with the love of the Holy Spirit, so that I too respond to love with love. Jesus became the true expression of the Father's love, and it is the Holy Spirit who will help me to grasp this total love, which is seen above all in the final sacrifice of Jesus on the Cross (Rm 5:6-8). Because he totally loves, he is prepared to die for me. Thus he demonstrates to the world that the Father dies for each one of us in his only Son (Jn 3:16-17). I need to try to realise the extraordinary, totally undeserved privilege which has been given to me. The Father has, first and foremost, given me life and only he can give life: 'All life, all holiness comes from you' (3rd Eucharistic Prayer). And beyond that, he offers me the gift of his friendship but leaves me free to respond or not, as I choose.

Neither of my parents could so much as shape one of my eyebrows. Only my Father in heaven can work the miracle of my creation (Ps 139:13) and I am the Father's 'work of art' (Ep 2:10).

The Father's dream and my desire

Just like every parent, God our Father has great plans, wonderful dreams for me, 'I know the plans I have in mind for you — it is Yahweh who speaks — plans for peace, not disaster, reserving a future full of hope for you' (Jr 29:11). His plans are for my happiness and he hopes these plans will be fulfilled in the eternal home his Son bought for me with his life (Jn 14:1-3). His dream is that I will become ever more aware that I am his son or daughter.

He has a different dream for each person according to each one's unique personality. Each of us reflects a different aspect of his Son and so each of us is called individually. Unless I respond and fulfil the purpose for which I am made, I will not fulfil myself as a human being. I will never quench the deep thirst that is at the heart of being truly human, a longing to be what the Father wants me to be.

God, you are my God, I am seeking you,
my soul is thirsting for you,
my flesh is longing for you,
a land parched, weary and waterless;
I long to gaze on you in the Sanctuary,
and to see your power and glory' (Ps 63:1-2).

I am yearning to become whole and fulfilled, for the image of the Father to become complete in me. Recognising my privileged relationship with the Father puts everything else into perspective. Such things as power, wealth, recognition, all count as nothing compared with the love of the Father who waits for me daily and who longs to hear my voice! I am like the Levite in exile; I cry out in my soul's thirsting for the Father:

'As a doe longs for running streams, so longs my soul for you, my God. My soul thirsts for God, the God of life; when shall I go to see the face of God?' (Ps 42:1-2).

Accomplishment

I can reach the presence of the Father only through prayer. In prayer, I not only seek to receive the Father's gifts, I also surrender myself to him.

'Deep is calling to deep as your cataracts roar, all your waves, your breakers, have rolled over me. In the daytime may Yahweh command his love to come and by night may his song be on my lips, a prayer to the God of my life!' (Ps 42:7-8)

The Father has provided me with an avenue into his personal and perfect love for me (Jn 14:). I am his child. In prayer, a re-creating experience, I become aware of how I am grasped by the Father and known and loved by him and so I can rise to new levels of friendship with him (Ep 4:23-2). My Father is willing to spend hours with me alone. He is acutely interested in my moment by moment activities (Ps 139:16-17). He, who made the universe, makes himself available to me.

In prayer, I imbibe the truth from the Spirit of Jesus that I am infinitely loved by my Father who lives in Jesus (Rm 8:1). Just to make sure that I understand his love for me, he sent me the perfect expression of himself, namely Jesus. When I look at Jesus, I can see my Father (Jn 14:7-9). When I go to him in prayer, the Father embraces me with his two hands, Jesus and the holy Spirit.

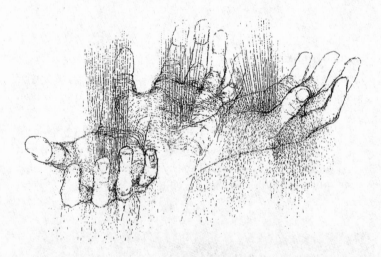

Chapter Three
Friendship: a Meeting

Encounter

When I meet someone else I change. My response to that person makes me different. I am either attracted or repelled, or perhaps simply uninterested. The same is true of that person's response to me. There is always a reaction when we inter-relate with another. If our meetings develop and our response to one another is positive, a friendship may emerge and we gradually grow in love for one another. I know my feelings towards the other person are feelings of love because the whole of myself is affected. On the other hand, I can only know of the love of another for me through faith and trust (1 Jn 4:16). If this is true of my friendship with another human person, then it is also true of my friendship with God. I can see examples of these friendships in the lives of Abraham, Moses, Mary and others.

Meeting God in prayer can be an awesome experience. In prayer I respond from the deepest part of my being, and try to be as open as possible. If God seems to be 'absent', it may be that like Moses (Ex 3:4-6) Jacob (Gn 28:16-17) and Mary (Lk 1:29-30), I might not be able to endure so unsubstantial a meeting with him, for God is purity and holiness itself (1 Jn 3:7).

Welcome or unwelcome

If I am aware of this purity and holiness I may be afraid and like Adam and Eve, I may prefer to hide (Gn 3:8-10). I can cut myself off from his friendship and try to live without him. We are all free to refuse the Father's love. Because God is love (1 Jn 4:8) he does not force himself on us. His love and respect for us are too great (Mk 10:21). However, if I try to endure the times he seems to be absent, if I keep returning that look of love and friendship that I experience in meeting Jesus, I may, with the help of the Holy Spirit, be able to leave everything and follow him.

I need the help of the Holy Spirit to turn back to God. I learn from Sacred Scripture that this turning back is an essential part of my relationship with him, and that God has constantly been calling his people back to himself: 'Listen, O Israel ... come back ...' is mentioned so many times in the Old Testament because his people were always turning away from him. When they did return, it was in order to 'seek the face of the Lord.' The more I turn back to God, the more I acknowledge my need for God to change me. So when God draws out and receives this response from me, it is expressed in repentance (Mk 1:1). The more I can say, like the Prodigal Son/Daughter, 'Father, I have sinned against you', the more aware I become of the Father always saying to me, 'You are a child of my love.' If, however, like Israel, I repeatedly fail to turn back to God, then gradually I will lose my sensitivity to the holiness and purity of God until finally I become dead to it.

When I allow myself to face the holiness and purity of God, I may well change. I may be able to see myself as I really am. I can change from being the proud person that I am into a humble sinner before God. Faced with God's purity, I become aware of my unworthiness to be in his presence; faced with his holiness I realise that, like the tax collector, I dare not even raise my eyes to heaven. I can only say 'God, be merciful to me, a sinner' (Lk 18:13).

Ever deepening friendship

Psalm 51.
An expression of true repentance: if I wish to pray and reflect on my need for true repentance I can use this psalm and make it my own.

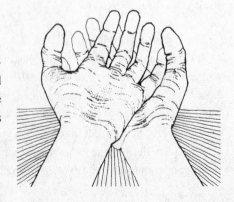

v 1. *Have mercy on me, O God, in your goodness, in your great tenderness wipe away my faults;*
My eyes must always be on God and not on myself. It is God who brings about true conversion of heart.

v 2. *wash me clean of my guilt,*
purify me from my sin.
It is the Father who forgives — only he can put things right. Only God, through his goodness and love, can wipe away my faults.

v 3. *For I am well aware of my faults,*
I have my sin constantly in mind,
Unless the Father works this conversion in me nothing happens.

v 4. *having sinned against none other than you, having done what you regard as wrong.*
If I can hurt another of his children, I have somehow been able to harden my heart and forget how important his friendship is to me. I see that the broken friendship is my fault, it is my heart that must be changed.

v 5. *You are just when you pass sentence on me, blameless when you give judgement. You know I was born guilty, a sinner from the moment of conception.*
The hurt of this broken friendship is something only the Father can heal through his forgiveness. It goes deeper even than friendship, for the Father has to forgive.

vv 6-7. *Yet, since you love sincerity of heart,*
teach me the secrets of wisdom.
Purify me with hyssop until I am clean;
wash me until I am whiter than snow.
The Father has to do so much; he has to make me whole again —I need the help of the Holy Spirit to show me the truth of my life.

vv 8-9. *Instil some joy and gladness into me,*
let the bones you have crushed rejoice again.
Hide your face from my sins,wipe out all my guilt.
Joy and peace are gifts from God and emanate from reconciliation.

vv 10-11. *God, create a clean heart in me,*
put into me a new and constant spirit,
do not banish me from your presence,
do not deprive me of your holy spirit.
To create is a divine action. It is the work of the Spirit of the Father.
Yet, I must do my part and offer my 'crushed and broken heart.'

vv 12-13. *Be my saviour again, renew my joy,*
keep my spirit steady and willing;
and I shall teach transgressors the way to you,
and to you the sinners will return.
God has come to us as Jesus, as Saviour, because he will save me from
my sins. Firstly, he will show me the way back to the Father and then
he will send me to bring others back to him also.

vv 14-15. *Save me from death, God my saviour,*
and my tongue will acclaim your righteousness;
Lord, open my lips,
and my mouth will speak out your praise.
This experience of liberation compels me to rejoice, and to praise God
for his goodness to me. It leads me to proclaim God's love and
compassion.

vv 16-17. *Sacrifice gives you no pleasure,*
were I to offer holocaust, you would not have it.
My sacrifice is this broken spirit,
you will not scorn this crushed and broken heart.
My part in reconciliation is small. All I have to do is offer my heart so
that the Spirit may work in me.

vv 18-19. *Show your favour graciously to Zion,*
rebuild the walls of Jerusalem.
Then there will be proper sacrifice to please you — holocaust and
whole oblation — and young bulls to be offered on your altar.

Jesus brings joy and peace because he liberates us from the consequences of our sin. Although he shows the way to repentance, the primary message is one of ioy and hope. These gifts of joy, hope and sorrow, all come from God (Ezk 36:26), but they are not to be confused with ordinary joy or feelings of self-pity. Divine joy is the joy of reconciliation, it tells us we are never beyond redemption. Although Peter betrays Jesus, Jesus looks straight at Peter (Lk 22:61-62). Because it is a loving, forgiving look, with no hint of reproach, Peter is able to recognise the generosity of this love — a love which he knows he does not deserve — and therefore the enormity of his betrayal. He goes outside and weeps bitterly. Together with the gift of repentance Peter receives the gifts of deep peace and Joy.

All such experiences are granted to me by the Spirit of God and so I must look to God to give them to me (Ep 1:17-19). Because I need to see that I am not self-sufficient, I must always ask God to help me see my need for him. 'By Your light, we see light.' (Ps 36:9)

Chapter Four
God the Father: Prodigal of Love

The sickness of sin

Unless people are aware that they sin, Christianity is operating in a void and scripture has no meaning or purpose (1 Jn 1:8-10). Jesus reveals that everyone sins, but also that he has been sent by his Father to make us free (1 Jn 4:10). Without him there is no freedom, 'for cut off from me you can do nothing' (Jn 15:). St John makes it very clear that we must all regard ourselves as sinners when he says that if we say we have not sinned, then we are calling God a liar.

Sin is a disease, but before I can be cured of any disease, I have, first of all, to admit that I am ill and that I am unable to cure myself. People do not ask for the doctor until they realise they are sick. I can only be 'saved' therefore and healed from the injury of sin when I recognise my need. 'God, be merciful to me, a sinner' (Lk 18:13). Just as a doctor must recognise the freedom of the patient to accept or refuse the cure, so too, the Father allows me the freedom to decide whether I want him to heal me. Without help I am powerless even to recognise my need. I can blind myself to it. Jesus came to reveal to each of us, to me, the capacity I have to block out the Father's love.

In his letter to Timothy St Paul says:

'Here is a saying you can rely on: If we have died with him, then we shall live with him. If we hold firm, then we shall reign with him. If we disown him, then he will disown us. We may be unfaithful, but he is always faithful, for he cannot disown his own self' (2 Tm 2:13.

This is an excellent summary of the message of all the prophets (Mk 12:6). The mission of the Son was to show that the Father's love is greater than all our wickedness; that, though I have sinned, I am still accepted unconditionally. This truth is revealed through the fidelity of the Father's love (Jn 18:37); though the steadfastness of that love is a mystery. Sin, which is a rejection of the Father's love, is not easy to understand. It, too, is a mystery.

Jesus searches for sinners

When Jesus came, most people thought they already knew what sin was, but Jesus showed them that they didn't understand sin at all. Indeed, the Gospels show that Jesus has a special relationship with sinners. Sinners are human beings (children of the Father), and he seeks them out (Mk 2:17), because they are at the heart of his mission. He has been sent by his Father to search for sinners, not to instigate a social revolution, or to take sides with outcasts, or to sort out peoples' relationships with one another. Sometimes, his actual mission will contain these issues but they are secondary. Jesus' prime objective is to heal my relationship with my Father, to help me rediscover and re-vitalise this relationship.

Jesus healed the physically sick who were brought to him (Mk 2:3-4), but he did not deliberately seek them out even though at that time they were regarded as 'sinners'. Sinners were much more the object of his concern and it was he who took the initiative to show his genuine acceptance of them. He befriended prostitutes and publicans and did not hesitate to be seen in public with them (Lk 15:1-2). The object of his mission was to deepen the sinners' notion of sin and show them and each of us how little we grasp its gravity (Jn 9:40-41). It is important that we do. Even priests do not understand sin, although they think they do. In every age, the Church fixes on a particular sin, such as drugs, sex, theft or perjury, and in so doing overlooks the fact that such things were, and still are, only symptoms of the primary cancer which is underestimating the unfailing generosity of God's friendship and what his love can do for us. Until Jesus came, human kind was always looking for ways to remove the evil within itself and to make amends for the way evil had spread. Jesus enters into the midst of sinners, eating and drinking with them, and asserts that he comes 'from above' (Jn 8:23), to bring healing and forgiveness. Forgiveness comes from the Father, it is a freely given gift that we cannot earn for ourselves.

Jesus also reveals that sin is in all people, above all in those who consider themselves 'sinless'. He illustrates this in the Parable of the Pharisee and the Publican:

'Two men went up to the Temple to pray, one a Pharisee, the other a tax collector. The Pharisee stood there and said this prayer to himself, "I thank you, God, that I am not grasping, unjust, adulterous like the rest of humanity, and particularly that I am not like this tax collector here. I fast twice a week; I pay tithes on all I get." The tax collector stood some distance away, not even daring it raise his eyes to heaven; but he beat his breast and said, "God, be merciful to me, a sinner" This man, I tell you, went home again at rights with God; the other did not. For everyone who exalts himself will be humbled, but the man who humbles himself will be exalted' (Lk 18:9-14).

The Pharisee in this parable is a particular person, in a particular place. It is also I, here and now! There is a large part of me that believes that I can heal myself through prayer and penance, that by and large, I deserve or have earned God's love. Jesus showed this attitude to be absurd. As long as the Pharisee believes that he is on an even footing with the Father, he makes God superfluous. Because he thinks he understands sin, he thinks sin does not affect him. He doesn't understand that God's love is a gift. He thinks he has earned it. One needs to ask for divine wisdom to see how disastrous the consequences of this attitude are.

Sickness to health through love

There is another illustration of sin and forgiveness in St Luke's Gospel (Lk 7:36-50) and there are two ways of looking at it. The woman who was a sinner had anointed Jesus' feet with expensive ointment and, weeping, she wiped them with her hair. The Pharisee, whose house

Jesus was in, criticised him for allowing himself to be touched by a woman who 'had a bad name in the town' — obviously he feels this woman does not deserve to be loved, whereas he does. Jesus answers him by reproaching him for not daring to acknowledge their friendship publicly: 'You did not anoint my head with oil, but she has anointed my feet with ointment. For this reason I tell you that her sins, her many sins, must have been forgiven her, or she would not have shown such great lov.' (Lk 7:47). One interpretation of this is that because the woman sheds many tears and shows much love she is forgiven. She earns forgiveness.

A better interpretation is that the woman has already received the gift of forgiveness. She was sorrowful long before she shed her tears and this enabled her to show unbounded love.

Even as she seeks forgiveness, her eyes are opened to the lavishness of the Father's love and so she responds generously. The initiative comes from the Father and his forgiveness bears fruit in her, in the form of an increase in love and a better understanding of the truth of the Father's merciful, forgiving love. This could happen to us, too.

The woman who was a sinner illustrates the difference between remorse and repentance. Remorse is a monologue centred on itself, while repentance is a dialogue. In remorse I feel sorrow for myself, but I do not express that sorrow, and because I never express it, I tend towards self pity and become downhearted, and despondent. This is what Judas did. he did not believe that repentance and forgiveness were real or possible. Peter, on the other hand, showed true repentance; he verbalised his sins and was forgiven, and his confession was in terms of love. Look at the dialogue between him and Jesus: 'Simon, son of John, do you love me?' He (Peter) replied, 'Yes, Lord, you know I love you' (Jn 21:17). We are reminded of another dialogue when the younger son, in the parable of the

two sons, 'confesses' to his father saying: 'Father I have sinned against heaven and against you'. Before he can say 'I no longer deserve to be called your son, take me as one of your hired servants', his father interrupts him, saying to the servants 'Quick, bring out the best robe and put it on him' (Lk 15:21-22). The son understands that his father has always loved him in a way he has never recognised.

Confession is difficult simply because it is an admission that the Father's forgiveness is offered readily and unconditionally. It is very difficult for me to believe in and therefore to receive and absorb such forgiveness. It also takes time to be imbued with real acceptance in the aftermath of strong feelings of guilt. Intellectually, I know I have been forgiven, but it will take time for the damage I've done to myself to heal. I make the Father happy when I give him the chance to forgive me and to heal me. When I give God the opportunity to be God, I must look directly at the Father's love and learn how to celebrate!

Once I have been reconciled with the Father, I can be reconciled with my neighbour (2 Co 5:17-20). Once I recognise my own guilt and know I am forgiven I can even love my enemy (1 Jn 4:19-21). As long as I sin,

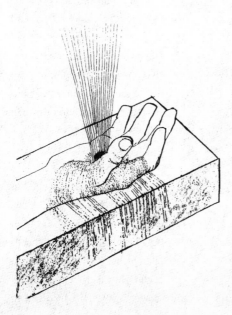

however, I will remain naive and shallow, and will not go far in the service of others. Sin inevitably leads to the Cross, to a need for reconciliation. The forgiveness experienced in reconciliation enables me to face my weakness and sinfulness without becoming despondent or depressed.

Jesus fulfilled his mission by openly accepting everybody he met, the tax collector, the prostitute; he found something good in everybody and condemned no-one (Jn 3:17). No one was too wicked in his eyes nor beyond his acceptance. When I feel condemned, my creativity, my power to love, my joy in life and my sense of wholeness, is blocked. When I come to understand, either suddenly or gradually that I am neither rejected nor condemned but accepted and loved by another on whom I depend, life takes on a different colour. I come back to life.

Jesus loves the sinner but abhors the sin

Jesus never suggests sin doesn't matter, but he distinguishes between the sinner and the sin. He condemns the sin and forgives the sinner, as he demonstrates in the way he treats the woman caught in the act of adultery:

Jesus was left alone with the woman, who remained standing there. He looked up and said, 'Woman, where are they? Has no one condemned you?' 'No one sir' she replied. 'Neither do I condemn you,' said Jesus, 'go away, and don't sin any more' (Jn 8:10-11).

Jesus condemns her sin, but he doesn't condemn her. He plainly calls her deed a sin, but does not write her off. Jesus doesn't merely say she is free, but he makes her free — free to change her behaviour and to regain her self-respect. His message is not merely verba, it is dynamic. Jesus exposes sin, by offering

acceptance and forgiveness. By our own standards, sin makes us unworthy of God's love and so we condemn ourselves. We feel we no longer deserve his love. Fortunately for us God does not employ our standards. God's love does not have to be deserved or earned. He loves us generously, whether we deserve it or not. God did not therefore demand a price for this reconciliation (Lk 23:34), but the world exacted the death of his Son because it resented having its way of life challenged (Lk 23:20-23). To be aware of the Father's love as revealed in his Son (Rm 5:8) is to become aware that there is no limit to the Father's love — it transcends all that is human (Rm 11:33-36).

I must ask for the grace to realise, not by reason, but through faith, my need for redemption - always and everywhere. I must acknowledge the gift of redemption because this is, above all, how he revealed himself as the Father, Prodigal of Love.

Chapter 5
Prodigal Son and Prodigal Father

Unconditional love

When Jesus was asked why he mingled with sinners, he told the Pharisees and the Scribes the famous parable of two sons, one 'prodigal', and the other 'dutiful' (Lk 15:11-32). The father loves his son unconditionally which is why the story is so hard for us to understand. Human love is always conditional. We feel love has to be earned, but the father in the story represents God, who loves us totally, forgives us unquestioningly even when we feel we don't deserve it. As I try to pray and enter into the meaning of this parable, I need to ask for the grace to realise the unconditional love the Father has for me. This realisation requires faith as well as reason because I find it difficult to accept and love myself. How then can God find me totally acceptable? Yet, we have to believe this is how he loves each one of us because Jesus tells us it is so and, indeed, demonstrates it by his forgiveness. Jesus came to reconcile us with his Father both by his teaching and by the love he shows indiscriminately to everyone he meets.

Jesus defends his association with sinners by telling his accusers that he is just like his Father; somebody who seeks out the lost and the sick. When Jesus sits at the table with tax collectors and sinners, the Pharisees ask the disciples ''Why does your master eat with tax collectors and sinners?' When he heard this, Jesus replied, 'It is not the healthy who need the doctor, but the sick. Go and learn the meaning of the words: What I want is mercy, not sacrifice. And indeed, I did not come to call the virtuous, but sinners' (Mt 9:10-13). I must pray to recognise my need for reconciliation and for God.

It is necessary to look at the parable step by step in order to understand how the Father's love is being revealed to me by his Son Jesus.

Father, prodigal of love

The Parable of the Prodigal Son, as it is known, could well be entitled: 'Father, Prodigal of Love'. Let us look first, at the relationship of the two sons with the father.

'A man had two sons. The younger said to his father, 'Father, let me have the share of the estate that would come to me'. So the father divided the property between them' (Lk 15:11-12).

Both sons were brought up by the same loving father but they represent two types of personality to be found in the father's house, and in the family of God. The elder brother is home-loving. All his interests and affections lie in the family home. The younger brother is more adventurous. All his interests and capabilities are directed outwards. His home surroundings are uncongenial to him, and he wants the free, fascinating, adventurous life 'out there'.

'So the father divided the property between them. A few days later, the younger son got together everything he had and left for a distant country' (Lk 15:12-13).

There was nothing extraordinary in a son claiming his inheritance in this way, and according to Jewish Law, the younger of the two sons would get a third of the property. What was extraordinary was the way the son spoke to his father. It would have been unthinkable in the society of Jesus' time, and his listeners would have been shocked. The father's attitude in the parable would have seemed strange too because they would have expected him to try to reason with the boy and perhaps even refuse his request. But Jesus' aim is to reveal the wisdom of God the Father (Is 55:8-11) and he achieves this by showing that the prodigal's father knows his son has gone too far but that he has to learn what it is like to live without his father's love. A place is a home because of the loving relationships it contains. If the love isn't experienced, it doesn't feel like home. He sees that letting his son go might be the only way to help him value his home and the love he finds there.

Learning my need for God

'… he squandered his money on a life of debauchery. When he had spent it all, that country experienced a severe famine, and now he began to feel the pinch, so he hired himself out to one of the local inhabitants who put him on his farm to feed the pigs. And he would willingly have filled his belly with the husks the pigs were eating but no one offered him anything' (Lk 15:13-16).

Jesus' listeners, while not approving the son's conduct, would have felt quite lenient towards him. I, myself, feel he got what was coming to him! (Pr 29:3). But, for the Jews, the tending and feeding of the pigs was quite another matter. The pig was the symbol of ritual uncleanness, and those who tended them treated with disgust. According to the Talmud, he had reached the very depths of defilement.

'Then he came to his senses and said 'how many of my father's paid servants have more food that they want, and here am I dying of hunger! I will leave this place, and go to my father and say: Father, I have sinned against heaven and against you; I no longer deserve to be called your son; treat me as one of your paid servants.' So, he left the place and went back to his father' (Lk 15:17-20a).

The 'conversion' of this younger son was really based on a sub-standard motive. He was starving and ready to eat anything. At this stage he was interested only in getting food (Zc 10:9), not in his father's love and mercy. This is precisely how I learn my need for God; when there is no-one else to turn to who can really help me; when, both externally and internally, I am on my knees in desperation, then I am the poor person with open hands before God (Lk 18:13), wanting whatever he is prepared to give me.

The loving father is always on the lookout for his returning son, and can recognise him even at a distance. 'While he was still a long way off, his father saw him, and was moved with pity' (Lk 15:20b). The waiting Father sees his Prodigal Son from afar and is anxious to welcome him home. Waiting is the measure of love, because the one who waits is saying that life is incomplete and so everything is on hold until the other person arrives. Prolonged waiting colours life; it tinges all the actions of the day with a hue of expectation and anticipation; everything else takes second place. This waiting is not inactivity but a stretching out, a yearning, a searching. As long as I have not obtained my heart's desire I will go on waiting and looking (Jn 20:11-14). The very fact that I am seeking and looking widens my ability to love and so makes the welcome greater and increases the joy it gives (Sg 3:2-4).

Deep love and trust

'He ran to the boy, clasped him in his arms and kissed him tenderly' (Lk 15:21).

A Semitic father would never have run, but always walked with dignity, perhaps hampered by the long robes he wore. He would have been obliged to gather them up if he wanted to hurry! So, when he ran, everybody would have known that something of immense importance was about to happen. Deep love does not bother about what other people think. His son had come home, even though every step on the way was an admission of failure and a reminder of his guilt. But he returned home because he understood something of his father's love. He realised that despite his behaviour his father would not reject him. He believed in a love much deeper and more faithful than his own. He had nothing to recommend him but his abandonment to his father, and his trust in his love.

'Then his son said, "Father, I have sinned against heaven and against you. I no longer deserve to be called your son." But the father said to his servants, "Quick! Bring out the best robe and put it on him; put a ring on his finger and sandals on his feet. Bring the calf we have been fattening, and kill it'" (Lk 15:21-23).

The son tried to stammer out his well prepared speech but never finished it, because the father hurriedly cut him off, asking for three gifts of incredible significance; a robe, a ring and shoes. Being clothed in these would immediately restore his son's dignity and indicate to the whole household that he was still to be treated with respect. He was his son. Whatever he had done was irrelevant because he loved him. These gifts might be compared to the three gifts Joseph received from Pharaoh (Gn 41:42).

The best robe was a mark of high distinction in the East. There is no mention of the son going to wash before being attired. This shows that the father wanted his son to feel accepted unconditionally. In addition, he may well have wanted to spare his son as much embarrassment as possible. If everyone else had to treat him with respect, it would help his son to regain his self-respect. This new image acceptance given by the father is sheer, free gift.

What a tremendous outpouring of compassion! The ring bestowed authority (Est 3:10). Having wasted a fortune, the son was now legally integrated back into the family fortune. Again, the ring symbolised the nature of their relationship, much as a wedding ring publicly demonstrates love between a couple.

What incredible forgiveness! The sandals, which were a luxury worn by 'free men' meant that the son must not go about like a slave. This gift represented mercy on several levels. Shoes signify a standpoint, a basic stance, a view of reality. A new view of himself and those around him was given to the son (Ep 1:18-19). He could not have achieved this for himself. It was freely given by his father.

What tremendous mercy! The fatted calf was a real luxury; the choicest prime meat. The younger son was really treated royally and he gradually began to understand the extravagance of the father's welcome and love, and the true meaning of forgiveness. It is then that he starts to experience real sorrow, because, he realises how much hurt he has caused his father who loves him to this extent.

What great generosity! 'We are going to have a feast, a celebration, because this son of mine was dead and has come back to life, he was lost and is found. And they began to celebrate' (Lk 15:23-24).

These verses show that the whole parable is welded into a unity. So, I cannot stop at the first half. Both describe the change: resurrection from the dead and the finding of the lost sheep.

> 'Now the elder son was out in the fields and on his way back, as he drew near the house, he could hear music and dancing. Calling one of the servants he asked what it was all about. 'Your brother has come' replied the servant 'and your father has killed the calf we had fattened because he has got him back safe and sound.' (Lk 15:25-27).

The younger son obviously stands for the sinner — so, who does the elder brother represent? I can find the answer when I consider the context for this parable, which is a reply to the charge of the Pharisees. Jesus is defending his conduct to the suspicious Scribes and Pharisees who are always ready to mock this kind of forgiving love.

> 'He was angry then and refused to go in, and his father came out to plead with him' (Lk 15:28).

The elder son was stirred by jealousy and resented the generosity of his father which he regarded as weakness. His feelings are dominated by what he thinks is fair or unfair. He has been dutiful and deserves to be rewarded. His brother has been wasteful and has forfeited his right to be treated as a son. He's had his share! The elder son has misunderstood what love is about. If he believes his father's love is something he has earned or deserved, he has underestimated the extent, the generosity of his father's love. But, the faithful and righteous son, by refusing to join in the feast, was as much in breach of Semitic morality and manners as the wild prodigal. In pleading with his elder son to join them, therefore, the father had to be even more generous and merciful than he had been to his younger son.

A parent expects to be obeyed — not to have to plead — but this father went the second mile (Mt 5:41). The elder son selfishly does not want to understand how his father feels about his brother. The limited nature of the love of the elder son is shown by his lack of generosity to his brother. He is so concerned with how his father's generosity affects him that he jealously and bitterly shuts his heart to the reconciliation between his father and brother.

'... but he answered his father, 'Look, all these years I have slaved for you and never once disobeyed your orders, yet you never offered me so much as a kid to celebrate with my friends. But, for this son of yours, when he comes back after swallowing up your property - he and his women - you kill the calf we had been fattening' (Lk 15:29-30).

Hurt and angry the faithful son launches into a tirade against his father. He stops using the respectful title 'father' and refuses to recognise his brother as brother. Instead, he calls him: 'this son of yours'. The elder son may have been a dutiful son, but he is not very loving. His love is limited; it seems to be conditional, depending on whether he feels his father behaves according to his own limited understanding of what is fair or deserved, so he is not able to be a loving brother. When he rejects his relationship with his brother, he rejects everything his home stands for.

My birthright as a child of God
'The father said: 'My son, you are with me always and all I have is yours. But it was only right we should celebrate and rejoice, because your brother here was dead and has come

to life; he was lost and is found (Lk 15:31-32).

Nevertheless, the father pleaded with the son. I need to listen to the tone of voice in the words as if he is addressing me: 'My son, (or daughter) you are with me always, and all I have is yours....' He loves both of them in their selfishness. He reaches out to his elder son, because he too needs his love as much as, if not more tha, the younger one, and gently reminds him that his younger brother, who was lost, is found and has returned home.

Most of us are quick to condemn the younger son and have a sneaking sympathy for the older son. This can help me understand my sinfulness, my lack of generosity. To love out of duty, expecting something in return bears no comparison to the generous and undeserved love God the Father showers on me. It is helpful if I recognise that sometimes I am like the elder son and sometimes like the younger one. Perhaps I am like one or the other at different stages in my life.

The more I focus on the action of the father in this story the more I will recognise that Jesus is revealing to me the terrific compassion, the incredible forgiveness, and the tremendous mercy of God, my Father. And this love is what I am constantly being offered no matter what I have done or who I am -

'Yes, God loved the world so much
that he gave his only Son,
so that everyone who believes in him may not be lost but may have eternal life' (Jn 3:16).

Chapter Six
Healing: Good News in Action

The healing Father

The healing acts of Jesus conveyed the message that he had to come to set people free. They were the Good News in action. People were being saved; the blind were given new sight, the downtrodden set free… (Lk 7:22).

Jesus was teaching that he is Life: he restores us to life (Jn 14:6). His Father had sent him as Saviour of the World (1 Jn 4:14), to show it is the Father's desire that his world, and his children should be healthy and not sick. When we pray for healing we respond to the Father's desire to heal us.

Jesus came to save the whole person, body and soul. Nowhere in the New

Testament does it say that Jesus came 'to save souls'. When he cured the paralytic he used just one action to manifest his power to forgive sin and his power to heal physical illness. In fact he puts both on the same level, he clearly sees the two as one, when he says: 'Now which is it easier to say: "Your sins are forgiven", or to say "Get up and walk"?' (Mt 9:1-7).

Jesus' practice of healing on the Sabbath infuriated the Scribes and the Pharisees, and his cures, far from convincing them that he was sent from God, only

made them see him as an impostor
who should be done away with (Lk
6:6-7, 10-11). The over-riding
motive for Jesus' actions was
compassion, to show God's love is
not limited to man made rules. Had
his miracles of healing been an
attempt to convince people of his
Godhead, he could have confined
his healing to the other six days of
the week.

His healing family

Jesus has given all his disciples
the power to heal. The gift was not

restricted to the Apostles. When he sent the disciples out (Lk 9:1-2; 10:1-
9), he was giving each one the power to preach the Good News as he
preached it: 'As the Father has sent Me, so I am sending you' (Jn 20:21-
23). He bestows on them the power to forgive sin, and to heal, and shows
us through Paul that we are sent out to preach, and to heal just as he did
(2 Co 5:18-21). By sharing his power with us in this way he can be
multiplied in us, his disciples, who, in their turn, can be his witnesses to
the ends of the earth. The Apostles used the same form of prayer,
producing the same effect, that Jesus used when they said 'Walk', 'Stand
up', 'Get to your feet'.

The Church, in the sacraments, uses a prayer that expects something
to happen simply because we have believed and prayed for it (Jn 14:12-
14). At the end of his Gospel, St Mark's writes '… while they, going out,
preached everywhere, the Lord working with them and confirming the
word by the signs that accompanied it' (Mk 16:20). This shows that the
Christian community continued to expect the power of healing to be an '
everyday activity of their community (Ac 10:37-38). It was by healing
people and setting them free (Jn 8:31-32) that Jesus demonstrated
salvation and forgiveness.

Healing in practice

When Jesus shared a meal, he showed his compassion towards people and exercised his power of healing in another important way.

In the time of Jesus, it would have been unthinkable for a devout Jew, let alone a holy man, to eat with 'sinners', tax collectors and prostitutes, people who knew that they had cut themselves off from God. By sharing a meal with them Jesus showed he accepted them. This is why his custom of eating with certain types of 'undesirables' caused such hostility throughout the whole of his ministry. When he shared a meal with an outcast, Jesus took away their shame, humiliation and guilt. By showing

that each person mattered to him, Jesus restored to each one a sense of dignity, which released them from their captivity (Mk 2:14). With these actions Jesus demonstrated the quality of his Father's love. During the eating of a meal — such was the social custom of the time — there would have been close physical contact (Jn 13:25) and it was this closeness that made a person feel clean and acceptable. They would have understood that the friendship of Jesus was a sign of God's friendship, since Jesus was recognised as a holy man. If people were acceptable to Jesus, they must be acceptable to God. The burden of their sinfulness, ignorance and uncleanness was taken from their shoulders, and no longer held against them. And, what's more, Jesus went further (Lk 5:30-32, 15:1-3), he actually entertained sinners! The outcasts were his invited guests! Jesus was certainly not a social climber. He entertained sinners in order to offer them peace and reconciliation. This was how he expressed his mission and his message — that was extended to all, even, perhaps most especially to the greatest sinners.

In wanting to heal people in this way, Jesus becomes vulnerable to them. We read in Matthew's account of the Last Supper that each of the

Apostles, his specially chosen friends, was capable of betraying Jesus (Mt 26:21-22). In the knowledge and light of betrayal most people become bitter,

but Jesus opens himself in Love even to those who betray him. Somehow it seems that the more that people reject Jesus, the more he is able to love them. When we are betrayed and rejected, we often react with violence and anger, whereas Jesus responds to such behaviour by transforming the hurt and offering love in its place. Jesus showed that it is possible to be hurt· and injured by others without becoming resentful, and fearful of being hurt again. His acceptance and letting go, calling for deeper love to replace the hurt, is like a miracle. We call that miracle forgiveness (Lk 23:34). Jesus wanted to reveal that this is what his Father is like (Jn 1:18). To love others totally and completely — even to the extent of being ready to die for them — involves great suffering. To experience the rejection, coldness and indifference of someone I love dearly is the greatest pain I can suffer (Jn 13:27). Jesus, knowing the inevitability of rejection still goes on loving (Lk 22:15). I have to ask myself: is such a love possible for me? Sinners, the most rejected in society, who received Jesus' invitation to eat with him, responded in love and were converted. Yet I, who know who he is, and eat his Body and Blood, I continue to betray him (Mt 26:2) and so I should pray for the gift to believe that despite my rejection such love is possible in my life too.

It is in the profound awareness of Jesus wanting to enter more deeply into the lives of the Apostles that each of them realises his capacity to betray him. Is such a love worthwhile? Could not the Father have proved his infinite love for each of us without such a total self-giving? Shouldn't Jesus have withheld his love when he experienced such rejection? (Jn 15:13). Despite his life being filled with all his works of love, and despite the suffering he endured, Jesus had few friends who really understood the depth and breath of his love, Jn 13:13. His own disciples, his closest friends were slow to learn and they too rejected him. How like them we are!

My understanding of love is shallow. I seem to be capable of only so much love, and even that is painful. In my weakness I need the Holy Spirit to remind me of how much love is possible. Jesus underwent the same feelings of loneliness, abandonment, frustration and failure, Jn 16:32, that we experience. Because he is prepared to enter into a close relationship with us, and because he calls us friends, because he shows us such great love, he is entitled to command us to love one another, Jn 15:14, 17.

Chapter Seven
Reconciliation: Sign of Healing

Be healed

The Sacrament of Reconciliation is not only a great sacrament of forgiveness, giving us peace, it is also a sacrament of healing.

The 'wound of sin', the inner wound, is a more recent concept in the Church. It is accepted that when I undergo an operation to restore me to good health, the wound inflicted by the surgeon has to be given time to heal, otherwise there will be serious consequences. It needs to be looked after and tended, otherwise I will not recover completely; the operation has no chance of lasting success without adequate aftercare.

The Church recognises the 'wounds of sin' and presents me with a sacrament 'bringing varied healing for the multiple works of sin ...' (Canon 978). For the sin itself there is 'divine forgiveness' that repairs — just as a successful operation cures a disease or mends a broken limb (Mk 2:5). For the wound of sin, there is 'divine healing' — which is just like a successful recuperation period (Is 57:18-19). The wound of sin causes a three-dimensional suffering: there is damage to my self-image, to my relationship with others, and to my memory of the past, and all this takes time to heal.

In Reconciliation I receive not just divine forgiveness but divine healing so that the damage of the wound may be overcome and I am left with only good 'scars' that, just like physical scars, will gradually fade.

Three-fold healing through Scripture

In order to co-operate with this 'divine healing', I can look to scripture to help me. Firstly, with regard to my self-image, I find that Jesus quotes

Lv 19:18: 'Love your neighbour as yourself' (Mt 22:39). I must love myself before I can love my neighbour; in fact the more I learn to love and accept myself the way God loves and accepts me, the more I realise how much I am loved, and, consequently, the more I can give myself to my neighbour. I need to pray using scripture, trying to discover myself in the words I find there, so that I really experience how the Father looks on me. I can insert my own name; for example 'This is my beloved Son/Daughter (John/Mary), in whom I am well pleased'. There are numerous passages that can be prayed in this personalised way, for example: Is 43:1-5; Jr 1:4-10; Mt 3:17; Lk 1:28.

Secondly, I want that 'divine healing' to help me to be capable of truly loving and forgiving others. I need to become better at healing relationships, and again I can look to scripture. I ponder the way Jesus forgives and loves when, in response to the criminal's request, 'Jesus, remember me when you come into your Kingdom', Jesus replies: 'Indeed, I promise you, today you will be with me in paradise' (Lk 23:39-43, Mt 27:44).

It is possible for me to ask Jesus to remember me, too. I can also listen to the question he put to Peter, not once, but three times: 'Do you really love me?' And like Peter, I hear myself reply: 'Yes, Lord, You know I love You'. In praying like this, I can become, little by little, more like Jesus in loving and forgiving and discovering that I myself am truly loved and forgiven (Jn 21:15-17).

Thirdly, I need to have the bad memories of the past healed. I may not be able to forget what has happened, but I can try to let go of all bitterness, and learn to trust and be trusted. I want to be able to say to God:

> 'What god can compare with you taking fault away,
> pardoning crime,
> not cherishing anger for ever
> but delighting in showing mercy?
> Once more have pity on us,
> tread down our faults,
> to the bottom of the sea
> throw all our sins' (Mi 7:18-19).

I want to be able to hear Jesus say to me 'Peace be with you, for those whose sins you forgive, they are forgiven' (Jn 20:19-23). I need to be able to believe the words of the Psalm and make them my own:

> 'As tenderly as a mother treats her children,
> so Yahweh treats those who fear her;
> She knows what we are made of,
> She remembers we are dust' (Ps 103:13-14).

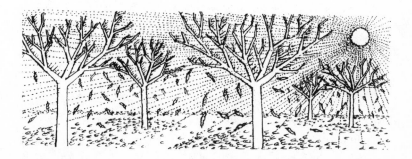

Peace be with you
The Church says in the prayer of absolution, 'May God give you

pardon and peace'. Pardon is for sin; peace is for inner healing.

Where do I find this peace? True peace is far more than tranquillity. Peace is essentially internal, reaching our inner self, whereas tranquillity is e x t e r n a l . Tranquillisers offer a superficial, transitory peace. At most they deaden the pain for the time being, but real peace goes deeper, Jn 14:27. It is not so much the absence of tension as the ability to live with that same tension or anxiety, and yet to be able to cope despite being powerless to change it. Peace is the fruit of love, and the work of Christianity is making that love universal, Mt 5:43-48, because none of us can fully enjoy peace until we all do. Eucharistic Prayer 3 asks the Father: 'In mercy and love, unite all your children, wherever they may be' — no one can be excluded from that unity!

Peace, therefore, is for inner healing. When I praise God the Father, I realise the enormity of my rejection of his love and I become aware of other things I do that reveal a poor response to his love, but now I can face them. To help achieve this I must pray for my confessor to be enlightened, Ep 1:17-19, and so discern my deepest needs. He does this through the Word of God and it is for this reason that it is so important to bring the Word of God, not just the sin, to the Sacrament. The Sacrament celebrates how the Word of God brings forgiveness, announces peace, and sheds light. The priest needs that light to discern the wound of sin, otherwise he cannot pray for inner healing for me, the penitent. The Father's healing extends to the whole person, therefore to avoid or by-pass the Word offered in Reconciliation is really a violation of the whole spirit of the new rite. (Better a few well-celebrated confessions than many hurriedly made ones). The gentle but direct ministry of the confessor allows the Holy

Spirit into the weakest areas of my life, where I am really hurt. Sadly, because I am ashamed and not certain that he loves me totally, I usually invite him only into those areas which I think are not too bad.

Jesus does not want any of us to ignore or rationalise away the sinful habits which burden us. He wants to free us from those habits, through his healing power which comes to us through this unique Sacrament. Only when we allow him to do this, will we be acknowledging that we know that God loves us unreservedly.

> 'If we say we have no sin in us,
> we are deceiving ourselves
> and refusing to admit the truth;
> but if we acknowledge our sins,
> then God who is faithful and just
> will forgive our sins and purify us
> from everything that is wrong' (1 Jn 1:8-10).

Chapter Eight
The Peace of Christ

Christ's peace

Jesus brought peace (Jn 14:27), but a risky, costly and vulnerable peace. He was, after all, a threat to both religious and civil authority — because he subverted all those securities on which peace, as the world understands it, is based.

He refused the security of personal possessions: 'foxes have holes ... (Lk 9:58)

He refused status and privilege: '... here am I among you as one who serves!' (Lk 22:24).

He refused to exercise power over others: 'the Son of Man himself did not come to be served but to serve...' (Mk 10:42-45).

He stirred up fear among those in authority, for he preached against and renounced those securities on which their peace was founded. His life and words exposed their fears which were directed against him. He also absorbed their violence, transformed it, and returned it as love and forgiveness. This is the victory of love over all the powers of destruction, a victory which we celebrate at Mass.

No ordinary peace

Jesus' way of life was too threatening also for the Apostles. Their fear caused them to betray him. When, however, the Apostles met Jesus after his resurrection, they could see in his eyes that they had his peace and joy and forgiveness (Jn 20:20). 'Jesus came and stood among them'. It was while they were still afraid, fearful and guilt-ridden, that he came, unexpectedly and suddenly, into their lives, bringing his peace. In receiving his peace, they received his forgiveness. They were aware that he had absorbed their sin of betrayal, and they were filled with the peace and joy of Jesus. Furthermore, he enabled them to pass on his forgiveness to others. 'As the Father has sent me, so am I sending you. Those whose sins you forgive, they are forgiven' (Jn 20:21-23).

If I am to experience this same peace and forgiveness, I also need Jesus to burst into my life: to come into my dejection, my sense of failure; I need him to bring me his peace. Sometimes he might do it by giving me the sense of his presence, as he did with the Apostles; at other times, he might do it through another person handing on his gifts (2 Co 5:18-20).

The price of peace

In the light of the Father's love for me my sinfulness is revealed. Just as it was in the light of the ultimate sacrifice of Jesus, in his death and resurrection, that the Apostles become aware of their betrayal. When I realise how great God's love really is, then I realise how mediocre my

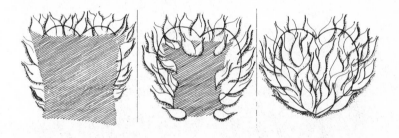

response is, or indeed how often I fail to respond at all. It is the same in my relationship with others. When, by a word or gesture, someone shows their love and concern for me, I may become aware that I have taken them for granted and hardly appreciated them. One instance can be sufficient to open my eyes to what is there all the time. Just as dirt or dust on a car windscreen is seen when the light of the sun shines through it, so the dirt and dust in myself are apparent when the light of God's love is allowed to permeate me (2 Co 3:18). The more intimately and personally aware I become of his love for me, the more my sinfulness is revealed (Lk 5:8). Just as love is a mystery, so my refusal of love is a mystery also. Sin, likewise, is a mystery. Forgiveness absorbs the refusal of love and passes

on a far deeper love, or love which not only gives but forgives. For-giving
is a mystery and forgiveness is the characteristic mark of Christianity. I
must become aware of my sinfulness before I can know that I need
forgiveness and the peace it brings. I have to know my need before I can
receive the love and forgiveness of God. It is essential that I be open to
receive, so that I can pass on to others the forgiveness of the Father, which
I receive in Jesus (2 Co 1:3-5).

The two criminals who were crucified with Jesus were affected by his
attitude to the crowd and his executioners. Even while they taunt him, one
of them recognises that Jesus is a forgiving man. Jesus is like a sponge,
soaking in the negative criticism, but somehow managing to pass on his
peace. As Christ was dying, his heart was touched by the criminal who
recognised who he really is. The criminal is rewarded with resurrection
today (Lk 23:43). Jesus was practising his own teaching.

True peace: fundamental, not superficial (Jn 14:27)

The rock on which peace is built is an awareness of the Father's
constant presence (Jn 16:1), no matter what happens. It is like a friendship
in which I know I am loved and valued as the person I am, with all my
faults. This acceptance is fundamental and total — it gives peace which
can survive all the ups and downs of life. Jesus promises this fundamental

level of peace which is crucial to me as a person. It is a peace which allows me to know that the Father loves me and accepts me totally as I am, which in time enables me to accept myself and to accept the love and forgiveness of other people. It is the kind of fundamental peace which survives even when the surface is in turmoil. Jesus did not promise a state of non-violence — nor did he say that our feelings would not be hurt. His more fundamental peace can contain wounded feelings: anger at injustice;

indignation at another's hurt that does not degenerate into acts of violence, aggression or self-pity. It goes beyond the immediate reaction and seeks to help the oppressed and the oppressor to be open to the love of the Father, who makes his rain fall on the just and the unjust alike (Mt 5:44-48).

'Leave me in peace' cries the teenager who is asked to turn down the music which is deafening everyone else in the house. Peace, here, is used in the world's sense, that is the power of a self-interested individual or group or nation to remain secure against any disturbance, interference or threat, even if the retention of that power is only possible through the exploitation, oppression or annihilation of other peoples. How different from Christ's peace is the peace the world gives!

'But now in Christ Jesus, you that used to be so far apart from us have been brought very close, by the blood of Christ' (Ep 2:13-22).

Through his death and resurrection, Jesus brought his gift of fundamental peace to his Apostles and to us. The cross is an 'I' with a line crossing it, a stroke through the I of myself. It is the most natural symbol of a love which unites two people.

The Holy Spirit of Jesus is a uniting Spirit who absorbs hatred, whose love is ultimately overwhelming because it initiates and brings to fruition the most maturing process in a person, especially when this love is directed towards one's enemies. Its complete unselfishness is powerfully illustrated in the commitment promised by two people in the marriage vows to take each other 'for better, for worse'. We are invited to love one another, not for what we can get out of the relationship, but for love of the other person, and in that way we can absorb rejection and, like Christ, give back love. If we rise to this challenge in our way of living and loving we will be filled with deep, fundamental, unwavering peace.

The one thing we all have in common is our humanity: to the extent that

we are drawn to our centre who is Jesus, so we will inevitably be drawn closer to one another. We are like the spokes of a wheel that are all turned towards the centre or hub. The spokes come closer to one another as they come closer to the centre of the wheel (Jn 12:32). In this common drawing together there will be no divisions of sex, race, colour, creed, but everyone united in Jesus.

Chapter Nine
Reconciliation: Sign of God's Concern

Sacramental prayer

The seven sacraments are seven moments in which we stand before God, our Father, face to face, and each time his gaze meets ours his response is different. All situations draw forth different responses: for example, a father will smile proudly as he watches his small child toddling across the lawn, but his face will change to concern if the child runs towards the pond. A mother will look with admiration and delight at its sense of adventure as her child examines everything within reach, but this delight will turn to fear for its safety if she sees her child putting its hand in the fire.

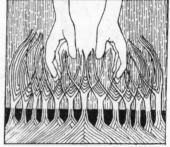

Similarly in a metaphorical sense, in the Sacrament of Reconciliation, the Father's face shows great concern for each one of his children in their plight. It expresses his anxiety and pain for the harm being inflicted on his other sons and daughters and on the damage that any of them have done to them-

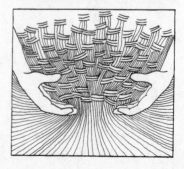

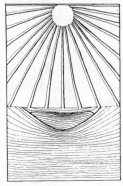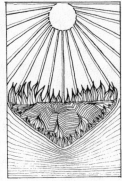

selves. This is how the Trinity meets us in this Sacrament, and it is this experience of the Father's forgiving love that the Apostles, the first to be reconciled by Jesus, were commissioned to bring to the world. The mission of the Church is a reconciling mission (2 Co 5:18-20).

But every sacrament is a formal way of praying, and the sacrament of reconciliation is a public declaration that I recognise that my actions have harmed other members of God's family and that I wish to ask their forgiveness and try to make amends. The sacramental way has a personal aspect, as does all prayer, but essentially it is where God and I meet publicly. In the context of the Sacrament of Reconciliation, God reveals himself to me in his Son (Heb 1:1-2), whom he calls Jesus, which means Saviour, because he is to save his people from their sins. I don't understand why God has chosen to reveal himself in this way — it is a mystery which I accept and try to live through faith (Is 55:8-11). There may be numerous occasions when my behaviour elicits God the Father's concern and there is no reason why I should not, each time, turn back to him and ask for his forgiveness privately.

Reconciliation, rather than penance, is the name given to this sacrament since it is supposed to convey a happy and joyful experience, an understanding that God's love is greater than my infidelities. I am spending time with God in a special way; I am meeting the Father, prodigal of love, who forgives me (Lk 15:22-24; 31-32), I am meeting Jesus, his Son, who is my Saviour (Mt 1:21), and I am meeting the Holy

Spirit who changes my heart of stone into a heart of flesh (Ezk 11:19).

Love that re-creates

Love is a freely given gift, a special grace which cannot be bought. Even the freedom for each one of us to refuse his love is, itself, a gift of the loving Father. he gave himself precisely so that we could freely choose whether to receive or to reject that gift.

The Holy Spirit is Love itself and our acceptance of this gift is basic to the fulfilment of the Father's plan for each one of us (Ep 1:4-7). Our life's journey, the life of the baptised person, is the journey of the child growing closer and closer to the father who gave him life. But this is a long journey (Lk 15:18-20). Being reconciled implies that a bond of friendship between two people which was broken is being repaired. But this reparation and healing is difficult and takes time. Two people have moved away from each other and there has been tension and strain. Gradually, the tension and strain ebb away and the two become more at ease with each other. Finally, there is reunion. However, the rift that has occurred cannot be eradicated automatically or instantly, but awaits a change of heart, for the nature of its pain is too intimate and too personal. This process cannot be hurried, it takes a long time, and the measure of the strength of the reunion and the subsequent growth in friendship, high-lights how deeply the beloved has been hurt.

While this reconciling is taking place between God and myself, I am becoming more and more part of that Body which is the Church. The sacrament of reconciliation helps me to remain part of this body because characteristically the Body is made up of people who are people of faith, of freedom and of penance.

People of faith: The Church is made up of people whose fundamental belief is that God loved them so much he was willing to die for them must, therefore, recognise that this is how much God values each of my brothers and sisters and until I too am ready to die for them, I do not love as he does.

People of freedom: I realise that I have been, as St Paul says, a slave to sin (Rm 7:14), 'hooked' on it, but now I am set free. I first had to recognise that I was 'hooked', and then look for treatment. Even when, like the alcoholic who is dried out, I seem to be 'cured' of my weakness, temptation is always there. I need to be continually watchful, doing penance, in order to grow in love (Mt 26:40-41).

People of penance: I need to keep in mind that I have not deserved the generous love that God the Father bestows on me unhesitatingly every time I return to him. In order to become more like him, more generous in my love for others, I strive to go against my natural whims and discover that the means necessary is the practice of self denial.

In the company of a holy person, a really fulfilled human being, my shortcomings are highlighted and so I find it easy to change (Jn 4:8-9; 11; 25; 28; 29; 42), and likewise through the process of Reconciliation I undergo a change of heart. (The Jews indicated this change by the use of a different name. Thus, for example the persecutor, Saul, became God's servant Paul.)

All the sacraments strengthen my friendship with God. With Baptism

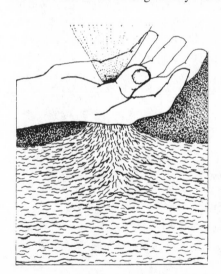

I am brought into his family and become his son or daughter. Through Reconciliation my friendship is repaired when his saving love rescues me, because he sees the harm I am doing, not just to his children, but also to myself. His generous forgiveness highlights the limitations of my way of living and so sorrow takes me over and begins to melt my heart of stone. God becomes not just Father, but the Father prodigal of love; Jesus becomes the Saviour who frees me and the Holy Spirit restores my capacity for love.

Despite the Father's eagerness to welcome me, I try to avoid meeting him in this Sacrament of Reconciliation. Perhaps my reluctance is due to the scrutiny this Sacrament demands deep into my being — into those areas which I try to hide even from myself. Yet I ought neither to fear nor to shun this Sacrament, because it is through this Sacrament that I obtain pardon and peace. These are the actual words used by the priest when he absolves me from my sin, 'Through the ministry of the Church may God grant you pardon and peace.'

Christ's Body is made up of all of us (Ep 4:15-16) and that is why a 'public' act of forgiveness is necessary. The Sacrament of Reconciliation is my public acceptance back into the family I had hurt and then left. Jesus says: 'Love your neighbour as yourself' (Mk 12:31). When I fail to carry out this commandment, even though I fail to love only one or two others, my failure to love actually affects the whole of the Church, all my brothers and sisters. It also affects me because slowly but surely I grow away from God the Father, separating myself from his love. At an earlier period in the history of the Church, sins had to be confessed publicly before the Bishop, who, to emphasise the grave damage done to the rest of the community, and the seriousness of the danger facing the sinner, would impose severe penance on those who wished to return to the community. No wonder so many people delayed confession until they believed death was near! In modern times to avoid public scandal and humiliation the procedure for confession is private, and one priest represents the rest of the community, but the rite is still performed formally on behalf of the Body of Christ — the Church. In the Sacrament of Reconciliation, the penitent and the priest represent the whole Church meeting the Three Persons. Despite the secrecy of the confessional, the sacrament is accepted as a public statement that we desire to love our neighbour, and that we wish to stay close to God's love.

This public act of sorrow, which asks the rest of the community for forgiveness, has two purposes, namely to fulfil the two commandments of love: 'Love God and love your neighbour — as yourself'. Its first purpose is to heal the rift, because forgiveness is not complete until reparation has been made to the injured party. But there is also the important element of healing the person who has inflicted the pain. By verbalising aloud the behaviour that I now recognise as hurtful to another, I am more likely to realise the damage I have done not only to another but also to myself, since my behaviour had de-sensitised me to the love of God. I also begin to grasp that without God's help I cannot change and admit that I need his love. This need has become a reality. I need to be liberated from sin since I am still a 'slave to sin' (Rm 7:14). I will never be totally cured but will always carry that weakness within me. I need healing and the prescription for it is the practice of penance in whichever form is helpful to me. Sin is my refusal to appreciate the love the Father shows me. Because of this ingratitude I do not allow God's love to permeate me, and that in turn prevents my loving both him, and my neighbour and myself.

In the Sacrament of Reconciliation, God's love is there to permeate me and give me new life; the more I open myself to his love's healing influence, the more will my own love increase.

Chapter Ten
To Act Justly

Sinful structures

We know, only too well, through the media, of the existence of terrible injustices in the world: the hunger, homelessness, poverty and deprivation experienced by the great majority of the world's population. Gradually, we are becoming aware that much of it has come about through certain unjust political and economic structures. They are unjust because they have been erected in such a way that the great majority of people in the world suffer poverty and deprivation, while a minority of people, largely those who have either erected these structures or who belong to them, grow in wealth, and enjoy a quality and standard of living which is steadily rising. We in the 'First World' are part of that minority, but we are becoming more and more conscious of our responsibility for the structures which give us so many benefits at the cost of grave injustice to others.

Until quite recently, when the word 'sin' was mentioned, it was generally understood to refer to individual sin, to the deliberate actions of individuals against God, others or themselves. It was committed with knowledge and consent and 'broke the law of God or the Church.' Now, however, we are aware of another dimension of sin, the social one — sometimes known as 'structural' sin.

Do I plead guilty?

In our world of today, I need to recognise and acknowledge the 'social' dimension of my sinfulness and my complicity in this present situation of injustice and exploitation. This awareness is a relatively new concept in the Church's consciousness but the understanding of the term 'sin' is being widened to include structural sin. I need to develop a greater sense of responsibility for the state of these unjust structures, so that I may repent of the sinfulness of us all and be instrumental in bringing about change. Inevitably, any structural change which relieves the suffering of the poor, either in the 'First', 'Second' or 'Third' Worlds, will necessarily involve a lowering of my standard of living and affect my access to opportunity. Am I ready, or even willing, for such a demand to be made of my generosity? I need constantly to turn to the person of Christ and ask the Holy Spirit to help me see how well I am following him — since it is only too easy for me to delude myself in all ways of sinfulness. I can defend, quite unwittingly, my use of privileges and possessions, believing I am using them properly, without recognising that my attraction to possessions and status easily and blindly leads me to aid the work of the devil (Mt 4:2-4). This can happen whether I am acting as an individual or as part of a group or system.

The power struggle

The contemporary meaning of temptation is enticing a person to do wrong or trying to persuade a person to take the wrong path. Temptation is like a tug of war, a contest within us to choose between looking after ourselves or looking after another. I can often feel equal to the challenge, ready to be put to the test, because I believe I am strong enough to withstand it. Paradoxically, it is when I feel strong that I need to be most on my guard, it is then that I can be tricked or deluded, because my gifts make me feel strong. They may well make me feel I don't need God's help in these areas. It's easy to recognise that I need him in my areas of weakness.

In the Gospels we read of the three temptations of Jesus in the desert as if Jesus himself is being challenged by the devil to a kind of contest. They are all about power. The Church is always being tempted to abuse its powers because although the Church has its divine Founder, it is at the mercy of our own human weakness, and, more particularly of those who 'lead' the Church.

He fasted for forty days and forty nights, after which he was very hungry, and the tempter came and said to him: 'If you are the Son of

God, tell these stones to turn into loaves'. But he replied, 'Scripture says: Man does not live on bread alone but on every word that comes from the mouth of God (Mt 4:2-4).

Christ is challenged, to use his divine power to remove the causes of physical hunger. But this would not be enough. The pangs of real hunger that Jesus came to appease are to be found deep in the heart and are not alleviated by material things.

The devil then took him to the holy city and made him stand on the parapet of the Temple. 'If you are the Son of God', he said, 'throw yourself down; for scripture says: he will put you in his angels' charge, and they will support you on their hands in case you hurt your foot against a stone.' Jesus said to him, Scripture also says: 'You must not put the Lord your God to the test' (Mt 4:5-7).

Jesus is being offered power which, it is implied, will enable him to make his mark. But power and the sensationalism that accompanies it were not what Jesus came to achieve. It is the hard road of service and suffering which leads to the Cross. And after the Cross, the Crown.

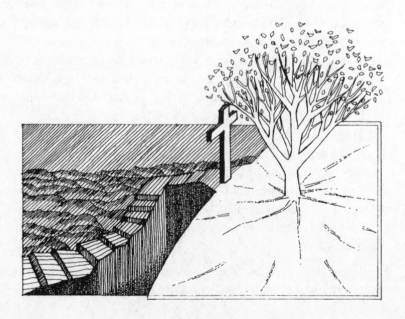

Next, taking him to a very high mountain, the devil showed him all the kingdoms of the world and their splendour. 'I will give you all these' he said 'if you fall at my feet and worship me.' Then Jesus replied, 'Be off, Satan!' For scripture says: 'You must worship the Lord your God, and serve him alone.' Then the devil left him, and angels appeared and looked after him' (Mt 4:8-12).

Here the devil tempts Jesus to compromise, he tries to persuade Jesus He can influence people by having power over them, rather than by serving them. But there can be no compromise in the war with evil, or with the standards of the world. Christian values are compromised in this manner when, for example, we suggest it is necessary to concentrate wealth in the hands of the rich so that increased investment will ultimately provide full employment and end poverty.

'Lord, may I act justly....walk humbly....' (Mi 6:8).

The aim and goal of every one of us as Christians, is to be like Jesus, to retain, or relinquish whatever we have, as God inspires us, and as seems better for his glory. I should seek what God wants, not what I want. The only reason for accepting or letting go of anything should be the desire to serve God, and to do so with increasing love and integrity.

This is extremely difficult and only God the Father can grant me this gift. Unless I obtain this attitude I will not recognise the nature and degree of my own complicity in the unjust structures of society today. I will remain blind to my own guilt, Jn 9:41. As Jesus tells us in his description of the Last Judgement, I shall even fail to recognise my own sinfulness, Mt 25:42-46. I need to ask the Holy Spirit to open my eyes to the gift God the Father is offering me, to enable me to retain or relinquish whatever I have for the glory of God, and for my brothers and sisters in need. This requires great inner freedom and I need to watch myself, to monitor my reactions because they will reveal where my heart lies. I must pray to be open to the gifts of the Spirit who alone can lead me away from my sinfulness.

Chapter Eleven
Looking at My Life: With God

Reconciliation

Reconciliation in its wider sense, is an experience which I should undergo regularly, even daily. It is not something to be experienced only in Church, or in the confessional. I need to practice reconciliation in every-day life, through my growing awareness of the Father's self-giving and forgiving love, for me and for each one of us. Jesus, his Son, is the human manifestation of that Love.

It is possible for me to respond lovingly to any given situation or person. Such a good and positive response comes from the presence of God. But there is also within me the possibility of a negative response, a withdrawal of love, which is not of God. Such a refusal adds to the confusion, darkness and pain that we call evil.

Sometimes my responses are confused and I am not always sure why I behave the way I do. What may appear to be love might, in fact, be my own selfish gratification. I need the help of the Holy Spirit to enable me grasp the truth about myself so that I become aware of the minor movements of my life, and able to identify what positive and negative forces are working within me. I need to cultivate the habit of looking reflectively at my life and how I live. This reflection is a kind of prayer which is on-going and its results are revealed by the way I live, as I become more and more loving in my response to people and events.

This kind of reflection is a most effective way for each one of us to find God and to recognise his hand in the happenings of everyday life. Nothing, however, is gained by constantly considering and re-considering my faults, and then turning to God to plead with him. The focus must be on God's love rather than on my weakness, remembering that God has been there from the beginning and everything good that is done is his work; his presence can be found even in failure. It is up to each one of us to wake up and notice him. One of the principal fruits of this regular exercise is the ability to be sensitive always to his presence in our lives. The most helpful way to approach this prayer might be to see it in the following five stages:

First stage

Every prayer is partly the work of the Holy Spirit, not just a human activity (Rm 8:14-17), and so I begin by asking the Holy Spirit to take me over and to enlighten me so that I can see things from his point of view (Rm 12:2). I turn to God and try to reflect on my day through his eyes. It is just like a human friendship where my outlook is coloured by the influence of my friend. I ask, not just to see the events of the day, but to see myself as he sees me. It is important to ask the Holy Spirit to take over my prayer so that I can see through his eyes. I need to look at things in a new way and that is not always easy. I need to come to see the good the Father did to me, for me, and through me, today. It may take a long time before my eyes are opened to this reality.

When we read the Scriptures we can see the hand of God in the events in the history of God's people. In Genesis 24:48, for example, we find the story of a servant looking for a bride for his master. He meets her and he blesses God for this experience. We too have experiences of God in all our undertakings and bless him for them. Slowly over the years I grow in understanding and I come to recognise God working in my life in an ever more profound way. Above all, I come to an awareness that God never leaves me, that he is with me all the time, in all that I do. I begin to see that everything is a gift.

God, as Three Persons, is always present, not idle, but working, and the good I do this day is what he achieves working through me. When I realise my poverty before God, that I come before him possessing nothing, then I can appreciate even the smallest gift and feel appropriate gratitude. It is the Holy Spirit who, gradually, will lead me to this deep realisation that all is gift. And instinctively and gladly I know: 'It is right to give him thanks and praise'! (Preface of the Mass).

There are many ways to express gratitude for all that is 'gift' in my life. I can show gratitude for my neighbour — the people I meet, work with and live with, my family, my partner, my community — by valuing them. They are the Father's gift to me. Children especially are the Father's gift to his world and their development is his concern.

I can show gratitude for whatever work I may have by working willingly. God the Father works through my humanity, just as he worked through his Son's. My ability to work, now, or in the past, in whatever way it may be, is something to be grateful for throughout the course of my life.

I can show gratitude above all for the gift of prayer, that relationship and friendship with God which is his life in me, by praying with openness and love, allowing his Spirit to lead me to a closer and deeper union with Jesus.

I can express my gratitude, for the gift of life, for the wonder of my being, through the words of Psalm 139.

Whatever gifts I may have, I have them by God's providence (1 Co 12:7) and his arrangement. Perhaps I am not inclined to see it that way, yet Jesus says he is working through me in every situation (Mt 10:20). I am his mouth and his hands, but it takes me a long time to understand this fully rather than simply 'know it' intellectually! In a way he puts me into the situation and then somehow he works through me. Jesus' main work during his life was as a village carpenter! Thus he lived a hidden life that was the gift of the Holy Spirit to him. Maybe I think of God as somewhere in the background just keeping an eye on me 'from the wings' so to speak, but this is not true. I need to remind myself that God's role in my life is much more central. If I do not see my work, however important or demanding, however unrewarding or menial in human terms, as God's work too, it is not surprising that I become bored and find work a burden! It takes faith and perseverance to see the hand of the Father in all the events of the day. In this practical way of prayerful reflection, trying to see through his eyes, I am led to a deep realisation that all is gift.

Second stage

It is a big challenge to me to find God in all things including, maybe especially, in my failings. Yes, even here I can encounter the presence of God. When I refuse the Father's love, albeit in the smallest incidents, I am aware of my failure to build his Kingdom. Unfortunately, all too often, I regard what I do as something I have achieved, rather than as the expression of my response to his call. Frequently my activity becomes my main pre-occupation and sadly much of the quality of my response is lost. I become self-motivated, self-moved, rather than motivated  and moved by the Holy Spirit. My activity itself can even be partly a refusal of God's invitation because I am not seeing clearly and I lack faith and therefore fail to live as a son or daughter of the Father. So, as always, I need to ask the Holy Spirit for guidance and help. Each time it is to the Holy Spirit that I must turn, since only in God's light can I see the truth — 'In Your light, let me see Light'.

Third stage

Here I want to look more carefully at how, if at all, I have been growing in love. I must take time to ask myself what has been happening in my life to try to identify the positive or negative attitudes that I have met in myself; have I in fact been aware of God's hand (first stage), and been able to see him working even in my weaknesses and failings (second stage). I might ask myself how did I meet Jesus, was it with fear or joy, misunderstanding and suffering, or harmony and peace; was I able to meet him, or did I turn away in despair, disappointment, self-concern, apathy or arrogance? Have I experienced a growing awareness of my sinfulness, do I rely on God to direct me or do I rely on my own judgement? How well do I know my gifts, since my weaknesses are the shadows of my strengths, how aware am I of those times when my gift has been misused by being withheld from others or used generously by being shared with others?

As always I can pray the Scriptures for enlightenment:

John 18:17 tells us how Peter denied that he knew Jesus. Peter's gift was friendship with Jesus. I look at 'the gift' with Peter; stay with him as he denies it out of fear and yet is drawn again and again to repentance.

Luke 10:40-41 shows Jesus at home in the house of Mary and Martha; what a tremendous privilege and compliment he paid them! I look at how Martha responds to 'this gift'; she resents the fact that she is not the centre of attention and Jesus meets her where she is.

In John 19:26 we learn that Jesus gave John to his mother as her son.

John was Jesus' favourite among the Apostles: 'the beloved disciple'. I look at how he responds to 'the gift'; he remains faithful to it.

Luke 7:47 speaks of the woman whose many sins were forgiven, because she loved much. I look at 'the gift' and see in her one who loves greatly in spite of her many sins.

Matthew 26:14 tells of Judas bargaining with the high priests before his betrayal. I look at 'the gift' offered to Judas, the choice of being one of the twelve; he can't appreciate it and so betrays the gift.

John 4:29 reminds us of the Samaritan woman's invitation to the villagers. I look at 'the gift' of the Samaritan woman, who was challenged to help Jesus. She allows her friendly nature to be used by him to spread the Good News.

Jesus is always there with me, giving strength to sustain me in my weakness. Even if my sins are the result of my refusal to use the particular gifts the Father has freely given me, he never withdraws his love.

Fourth stage

I am moved to sorrow in the face of the immense love that the Father shows me in spite of my ingratitude. My sorrow rises spontaneously as I realise the extent of my self-ishness. The Spirit of Jesus brings about this movement of sorrow in me (Ezk 36:25-27; Lk 22:61-62). Jesus looks lovingly at Peter, even though Peter has betrayed him. This makes Peter realise all the more keenly how he has re-paid this love. And so he goes out and weeps bitterly. Con-trition is not something I can achieve by myself. It is not depression or self-pity, but a living faith experienced, as I grow in the realisation of the Father's desire that I would love him increasingly with the whole of my being (Mt 22:37).

This sorrow leads to Christian joy: the joy of my being forgiven (Jn 20:20-21) and makes me into an ambassador of that forgiveness to others (2 Co 5:18-2). It is the fruit of listening to the Father through the forgiving Jesus.

Fifth stage

Now, strengthened by a greater awareness of the Father's love for me, gladly acknowledging my sinfulness and his power in my weakness, being truly sorrowful and yet filled with joyful gratitude for such forgiveness, I can look forward with hope. Now I know God my Father is always faithful (Jr 31:3). This faithful loving permeates me while I am trying to listen continually to him through his Son. He helps me to be less unfaithful for only God is faithful (2 Tm 2:13). The more I turn to him, who is faithful and forgiving, the more I become like him and so I confidently grow in hope. Hope for my future, and that of the whole family of God. This is a hope that stems from human weakness and transforms it into strength (Ph 3:13-1).

Chapter Twelve
Reconciliation: Sign of Christian Fellowship

Forgiving loving

Divine forgiveness belongs to God and not to us. When God forgives, it is always he who takes the initiative, and thus shows us how true forgiveness can come about (Lk 6:36-37).

Love is deepened through the process of reconciliation and forgiveness. It is only when we have begun to know the true meaning of love and friendship that it becomes possible for us to forgive in return. Any friendship is a gift, from one person to another. It is something completely undeserved. When that gift is offered me, all I can do is to accept it gratefully and try to respond. I cannot know in advance its effect and consequences, but if this friendship is deep it will affect the whole of my life and colour my outlook.

The deeper the friendship the more vulnerable I become, because the more I invest in a friendship, the more I can be hurt by my friend's response. If I have arranged to meet someone I know slightly and he fails to turn up for the appointment I am puzzled, and probably rather annoyed. However, if I have arranged to meet a great friend, and I have been looking forward to our time together, and he fails to turn up, and there is no phone call or explanation, at first I am worried, and then deeply hurt at the way I have been treated. I feel used and rejected.

What happens the next time we meet will depend on the depth of love between us. If my friend recognises my hurt and can explain the situation, and I accept and respond, then forgiveness and reconciliation will follow. I will appreciate the reason for the lack of contact and accept my friend totally with an even deeper love than before. There is a more profound insight on both sides, and so the friendship develops and grows.

A challenge to greater loving

Growth can be painful and we are inclined to avoid it if at all possible. When we hurt one another as loving friends, it is only too easy to minimise the acts of thoughtlessness and say 'It doesn't matter', or, for me to be so wrapped up in my own feelings that I fail to see or to hear the hurt, or difficulty, that my friend is experiencing.

In a truly loving and ever deepening friendship I gradually think less and less about myself and am able to give myself unselfishly. Even when my friend and I have hurt one another we can experience true sorrow and learn to face the truth that what has happened does matter. Forgiveness insists on the truth, even when it appears to be sharp, painful and harsh.

When someone I love, a friend or even a relative stranger, behaves in an unacceptable way, I do not need to accept the behaviour, even though I still accept the person. The same is true for me when I behave in an unacceptable way. I do not, nor should I, allow myself to 'get away with it'. My weakness, my pomposity, my ambivalence need to be challenged, even exposed to me by those who love me (Mt 10:20). This is very important as real criticism, positive comment and observation said with love can draw me deeper into God, who is love. Accepting criticism is not comfortable, indeed it can be very painful, but, living with Jesus of Nazareth is neither comfortable, nor painless. Yet, such an exchange within a loving relationship has the unique and great consolation of total acceptance — of a love that will not fail (Is 54:6-10). Forgiving love, therefore, is the fruit of real Christian sorrow, and flowers between two human beings as they help each other grow in Christian friendship. See the Letter to Philemon.

The world of today stands in great need of forgiveness, reconciliation and healing. It is so rare that when a father was able to say: 'I forgive you' to the terrorists whose bomb killed his daughter, he immediately became a household name and an ambassador for peace. When a woman said that she had forgiven the man who raped and abused her, it made national headlines and gave our torn world a truly Christian witness.

Reconciliation, as a ministry, is much in demand, not only formally and publicly but privately between individuals (Mt 6:12; 18:32-33). Living as we do in a climate of so many broken relationships we need help and guidance and, above all, the ex-

perience of a loving Father who forgives us all our sins and accepts us

totally and unconditionally no matter what we do. This joyous good news
of the Father's forgiveness can only be experienced as it is lived and
shared by you and me and all his sons and daughters throughout the world
(2 Co 5:17-21).

Chapter Thirteen
The Joy of True Relationship

The joy of laughter

It is said that people have lost their sense of sin, but all around me, I am aware of the sense of failure; the loss of innocence, the ugliness of greed and how these alienate us one from one another. There is a great desire for self-understanding, including a reviewing of past behaviour, and with it comes a tendency to brood over the past and a turning in on oneself rather than to reflect with the Lord. One can easily take oneself far too seriously. Because of one's insecurity,one can forget to laugh at oneself. We forget that Jesus is risen, he makes it possible for us to laugh, because he has freed us. Some people have been able to go singing to their deaths, and Thomas More actually joked with his executioner!

If I cannot laugh, it is not only because I have lost my sense of humour, but also because I have lost my inner freedom. When I give up spending time with God, I lose touch with God, and gradually I become dissatisfied and eventually depressed. By losing touch with God I have let go of joy. God is responsible for my joy; he is the source of it, for God is joy.

The joys of life

The humble human joys of my life, the confidence of knowing I am loved by God and by others, the satisfaction experienced in seeing the beauty of things around me, endow me with 'inner freedom'. This truth will make me free. The everyday joys, when they become more apparent, are like the seeds of truth gradually transformed into reality. Jesus shows us this when he says 'Look at the birds in the sky' (Mt 6:26-28) and 'think of the flowers growing in the fields.' Again, witness the joy of a father embracing his child come safely home (Lk 15:20-24), or a woman with her new-born baby (Jn 16:21-22). These are real, profound experiences of joy because they are for Jesus signs of the joy of the Kingdom of God. Above all, Jesus finds joy in seeing someone converted (Lk 19:5-10), or a friend demonstrating his trust in him, 'My Lord and my God!' (Jn 20:28).

The joy of Jesus

It is very significant that it is during the Passion that Jesus speaks to us of his joy (Jn 16:20-22)— the mystery of his death and Resurrection. The joy he refers to is the fruitfulness of his death by which he achieved our reconciliation with the Father (Jn 20:22-23), and with one another (Jn 20:17). By his death and Resurrection Jesus brought us peace(Jn 20:21) and introduced us to a new friendship with the Father (Ep 2:12-18). Living the Easter story gives new life to each of us. A life of friendship in the Three Persons, and a bond of unity and peace with others (Ac 2:42-47).

This is what Christian joy is all about. It is not an easy contentment nor a shallow self-satisfaction, but rather, a sadness overcome — that sadness which falls on me when I have said 'no' to God, when I have withheld love; that is, when I have dehumanised myself. Tremendous is the joy that is felt when I break free from such a burden and allow myself to become human again.

When the apostles meet Jesus after the Resurrection and first receive his forgiveness, they experience peace and joy. They become aware of the absorption of their sin of betrayal and denial, and conscious of the passing on of good when Jesus says 'Peace be with you'. Because they experience forgiveness and joy, they can pass this on to others; they would not be able to pass on what they did not possess. Peter, above all, knew Jesus loved him in his weaknesses and in his strengths, and it is in his deepening awareness of that forgiving love that he grows in Christian sorrow, a sorrow that always leads to peace and joy.

The pain of unselfish love and the cost of trying to live with it, is amply compensated for by the profound joy of realising I am loved for myself: that God loves me exactly as I am, warts and all. No wonder forgiveness is the characteristic mark of Christianity, for the mission of the Church is fulfilled when we realise that none of us loves enough; we are all sinners, and have need of the peace and joy of the Lord. Jesus, by his death and Resurrection, won that peace and joy for us: 'the disciples were filled with joy when they saw the Lord' (Jn 20:21).

The joy of the Apostles

The only time the Gospels tell us that the apostles were filled with joy when they saw the Lord was on Easter Sunday night. In the midst of their sadness and dejection, Jesus came to them and brought them joy. I feel sad when I am lonely and sense the emptiness of my life. But my faith consists in the belief that Jesus can fill that emptiness. He can bring me back to life just as he brought the Apostles back to life on Easter Sunday night. He filled their lives with the fullness of life and love (Jn 10:10-11).

The Easter joy they experienced was the fruit of the love of God poured into our hearts by the Holy Spirit (Rm 5:5). Jesus came to show the extent of the Father's love for me (Jn 3:16). 'A man can have no greater love than to lay down his life for his friends. You are my friends, if you do what I command you.' (Jn 15:13-14). This, in fact, is the source of my Christian joy and it is the work of the three Divine Persons within me. It is summed up in the words of Eucharistic Prayer IV:

And that we might live no longer for ourselves but for him, he sent the Holy Spirit from You, Father, As his first gift to those who believe, to complete his work on earth and bring us the fullness of grace.

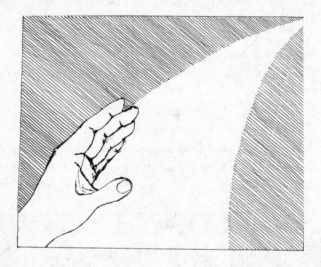

Chapter Fourteen
Rejoice with Me

Parenthood

One of the greatest joys a human being can experience is to become a parent. When a child gives its first smile in response to its parents, it is the start of a loving communication which deepens as the child grows

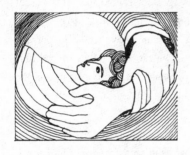

older. The first word, the first step, bring great love, pride and joy to the face of any parents who love their child. But this look may change to concern if the child toddles towards danger of any kind, and the parents will rush to save the child who may be unaware that anything is wrong.

If this is so for those of us who are human parents, then it is even more so for God, who is Father to each one of us. He is Father to me (Ep 3:1), who am his child, made in his image and likeness (Gn 1:27). I am his adopted child through Baptism and he loves me far more than any human parent ever could (Is 49:15). Sometimes, however, like any child, I am inclined, throughout my life, to run into danger, hurting and wounding myself and others, and so I am in great need of his love and care. Naturally, as he looks at me, the Father's face wears an expression of concern and he stretches out a hand to help me. In his redeeming love he sends me his Son, because he is a loving Go (1 Jn 4:10), who wants to save me from harming myself and others. For this reason he asked Joseph and Mary to call his Son, 'Jesus', which means 'Saviour' (Mt 1:21).

Jesus was a person like us in all things but sin (Heb 4:15). As an individual growing up, I have learned standards of behaviour and ways

of relating to others, and I have discovered that I can hurt people, not just by what I do to them, but also by what I fail to do to them, and for them. I can be hurt myself, too, by what others do to me, and also by what they fail to do to me and for me. We adopt certain standards of behaviour and forms of relationship which most of us recognise and accept as normal. But, Jesus says: 'Be perfect as your heavenly Father is perfect' (Mt 5:48). If I am following Christ and calling myself Christian, I have to go beyond the 'norm' and take that further step. For an extraordinary way of loving is asked, even expected, of me. I am supposed to love other people in the same way that God the Father loves them!

Jesus gave concrete examples of how to do this.

But I say this to you who are listening: Love your enemies, do good to those who hate you, bless those who curse you, pray for those who treat you badly. To the person who slaps you on one cheek, present the other cheek too; to the one who takes your cloak from you, do not refuse your tunic. Give to everyone who asks you, and do not ask for your property back from the one who robs you. Treat others as you would like them to treat you. If you love those who love you, what thanks can you expect? Even sinners love those who love them. And if you do good to those who do good to you, what thanks can you expect? For even sinners do that much. And if you lend to those from whom you hope to receive, what thanks can you expect? Even sinners lend to sinners to get back the same amount. Instead, love your enemies and do good, and lend without any hope of return. You will have great reward, and you will be sons and daughters of the Most High, for he, himself, is kind to the ungrateful and the wicked. (Lk 6:27ff).

Jesus gives me an extraordinary illustration of the depth of loving he is expecting. his commandments here are all positive and leave no room for compromise. Jesus expects me to go further than what is the norm for many ordinary 'good' people. I am called to love other people far more that is generally expected — 'If you do good to those who do good to you, what thanks can you expect? For even sinners do that much …' Jesus shows me through his own example that this extraordinary way of loving is the deepest form of love, namely 'forgiving' love.

On the Cross, Jesus said, 'Father forgive them, they do not know what they are doing' (Lk 23:34). What an extraordinary love Jesus shows towards his persecutors even as he is dying. As one of his followers this is the way I am expected to live and die! The manner in which Jesus continued to love even to his death is beyond our comprehension, because his ways were not ours (Is 55:8-9). It was no easier for Jesus to live in love than it is for us, even though he was the Son of God. We must never forget that he was a man like us in all things but sin. He sweated blood when he realised what lay ahead of him because he was terrified.

Being human, as we are, it was possible for Jesus to misjudge a situation as he did, for example, when, as a thoughtless 'teenager', he worried his parents when he stayed behind in the Temple (Lk 2:46-50). Similarly, through inexperience, he miscalculated when during his first mission in his home town of Nazareth he claimed to be the Messiah. This was blasphemy and it is not surprising that people tried to kill him (Lk 4:16-30). He had to mature like the rest of us and grow 'in wisdom and grace before God and people' (Lk 2:52).

Enlightenment by the Holy Spirit
Jesus, himself, asked the Holy Spirit to help him 'put on' the mind of his Father. Although he was without sin, he needed to pray the Psalms of repentance in order to understand the mind of his Father.

We know that when he was tempted in the desert (Mt 4:1-10), temptations which Jesus must have experienced many times in his life, he had to choose between enjoying the wealth, glory and power of a political messiah, or suffering the poverty and humiliation as the Saviour Messiah. The choice that he ultimately made, of relying utterly on God, shows that he was thinking more and more like his Father. But it was only as a mature man that he could see clearly what God was asking of him.

Paul, in writing his letter to the Christians in Ephesus (Ep 1:17-18) asks that the Holy Spirit would enlighten their minds, because he maintains that they need this new mind in order 'to know what God wants' (Rm 12:2). If I want to become like Christ (Mt 5:48), I must pray to have his mind and heart so that I may become perfect. Jesus himself said: 'You must be perfect, just as your heavenly Father is perfect'. I must ask the Holy Spirit to help me, so that this is what I desire.

In order to achieve unity with my sisters and brothers in Christ, I must 'always consider the other person to be better than myself' (Ph 2:1-11). Because I am still learning to think as God would have me think, because my mind is not yet sanctified, because I do not see the whole picture but only what affects me, I often make mistakes which hurt other people, and I need their forgiveness. I need to recognise that much of the time, when others hurt me, they do not realise what they are doing either.

When I pray the words of the Our Father 'Forgive us our trespasses as we forgive those who trespass against us', I am actually asking the Father to forgive me, only to the extent that I forgive others.

In the story of the Prodigal Son, the elder brother has not yet learned to forgive and so is unwilling to join in the celebration feast to welcome home his brother (Lk 15:28). By withholding his love, he renders himself powerless to enter into Heaven, which is always represented in the Gospels by a celebration meal. Even though his father begs him to join them, he still refuses. How vulnerable a father is to his child's response to love! God the Father is helpless; he cannot force us to love, or to respond to love, no matter how much he loves us. Yet those of us who have experienced his forgiveness, do have an understanding of how to love. The elder brother, who was not aware of being forgiven, or receiving forgiveness, or even needing forgiveness, had not had the experience of forgiveness and therefore had not yet learned forgiving love. He thinks in terms of a love that has to be earned. This is why he cannot understand why his father still loves his brother (Lk 15:20-30).

I can relate the parable of the Prodigal Son to the account in Luke's Gospel of the woman 'who had a bad name in the town'. Having heard that Jesus was dining with the Pharisee, she brought with her an alabaster jar of ointment. As she sat at his feet weeping, her tears fell on his feet and she wiped them away with her hair. Then she covered his feet with kisses

and anointed them with the ointment. Jesus says: 'her many sins must have been forgiven or she would not have shown such great love' (Lk 7:36-50).

Heaven is represented by feasts which are a celebration for those who have learned about forgiving love, those who have understood just how much they are loved by God the Father, those who want to be like him. It seems, however, that we have to be lost in order to experience what it is like to live without God's love before we can really appreciate it, as in the Lost Sheep Parable: 'And when he found it, would he not joyfully take it on his shoulders and then when he got home, call together his friends and neighbours? 'Rejoice with me,' he would say 'I have found my sheep that was lost.' (Lk 15:5-6). This is also what happens in the story of the Lost Drachma: 'And then, when she had found it, call together her friends and neighbours? 'Rejoice with me,' she would say 'I have found the drachma that I lost.' In the same way, I tell you, there is rejoicing among the angels of God over one repentant sinner' (Lk 15:9-10).

The importance of forgiveness in the life of a Christian is emphasised in the number of times it is brought into the Mass.

In the Penance rite we, the Father's family, ask forgiveness of God and one another. At the Kyrie Eleison, we beg 'Lord have mercy'.

The priest prays before reading the Gospel 'Purify my heart and my lips that I may worthily proclaim the Holy Gospel'. Later he washes his hands before the prayer over the gifts, and says 'Lord wash away my iniquity, cleanse me from my sins'.

When we recite the Our Father, the climax is 'Forgive us our trespasses, as we forgive those who trespass against us'.

At the Sign of Peace, we show our willingness to be united with one another, because we all belong to God's family.

At the Agnus Dei, we recognise the Lamb of God as the one able to take away our sins.

At the end of the Mass, being reconciled to one another, we are sent out to bring peace and joy to the rest of the world, Mt 28:19-20.

Chapter Fifteen
Reconciliation: Preparing for a Public Sign

Confession is a prayer of worship and thanksgiving, a recognition of that special love which God the Father has for me. It is only in the context

and power of that love that sin exists at all. Until I have felt, or tasted, or seen God my Father's love for me, it is not possible for me to sin (1 Jn 4:8), because sin is a refusal to accept or respond to that same love.

Confession is, above all, the discovery of what love is, and what it means to love. It is a song of praise to God the Father.

So often I have said, and maybe I still say 'I have nothing to confess', because I think I have done nothing wrong. Yes, confession is not primarily about wrong-doing. As with the prayer of the examination of conscience, or consciousness awareness, the first thing is to find something to sing about. Then I can confess that (Rm 5:8) and discover the love I have received and become more and more aware of i (1 Jn 4:10). So, I should begin my preparation for the sacrament, by focusing on a particular, concrete example of the Father's love shown to me since my last meeting with him in this sacrament.

This example will be the centre of thanksgiving in the actual celebration of the Sacrament of Reconciliation. Thanksgiving has not always been our first approach to confession and even in our prayer generally. In personal prayer, particularly, thanksgiving and praise can often be neglected. More often than not, I am reluctant and slow to see God's action and love in the world and in me. It seems easier to concentrate on darkness and destruction, even though I know it leads only to despair and death. When I look at the wonder of God's creative action in the world and in my own life, I become filled with wonder, praise and thanksgiving. I

am also filled with a desire to respond to such love and become increasingly aware of my lack of response. I want to be different, to change for the better. This is why it is so important to begin positively, when receiving this sacrament.

The next part of my preparation is to ask the Holy Spirit for guidance and light, so that I become aware of my ingratitude in receiving the Father's gifts. The Holy Spirit will not only help me to see how my actions are withholding love, and how I am deaf to his call, but also open my eyes to the blind areas of my loving (Jn 9:40-4), where I fail to 'put in love where love is not'.

It is helpful to look at the gifts which he has bestowed on me, and then I can see whether I have responded to the Father's love by sharing my gifts with others or by withholding them. I will enjoy a different relationship with God at different stages in my life, because my understanding and experience of love at seven years of age will be very different from when I am twenty-seven, and again when I am seventy-seven.

The Father called me at Baptism to follow him in love and since that moment my relationship with him has developed in different ways. He has called each of us to a particular 'state' in life. Either to marriage, or the single state, or perhaps to the priesthood or religious life. Maybe I am still discovering what state in life I am called to. Wherever I am, at whatever stage on my journey, my way of being and acting will alter accordingly. In each different circumstance I will have different relationships, relevant to my particular age and state. I will also have a very different perception of myself, of others and of God. I should be constantly growing in understanding of myself, with all my gifts, limitations, strengths and weaknesses. Here are some examples of the way different people examine their conscience according to their age and state in life:

A seven year old

(This could be used as a preparation for the Sacrament of Reconciliation or as part of the child's prayer at the end of each day.)

I look back on this day and I thank God for my family, my friends, for all the animals. I thank him especially for my Mum and Dad. I thank him for all creation, for animals, trees, plants and flowers. I thank him for the food I have to eat. I thank him for my friend who came to my house to play.

Now I try to think of the times when I have not loved Jesus today, when I have hurt others.

I think of my friends. I tell Jesus I am sorry — I am sorry for saying that I hate my friends when they call me horrible names. I am sorry for calling my friend horrible names. I am sorry when I upset my friends by saying things about them like 'I don't like you'.

I think of my family. I am sorry I punched my brother and pulled his hair I am sorry that I kicked my sister — I will try not to do it tomorrow. I will try not to fight with my sister and make my Mum cross. I am sorry for being mean to my Mum, when I stamp my feet and slam the door.

I think of my school. I am sorry for making a fuss about what I'm given to eat or having to do my homework

I tell Jesus I am sorry in my own words — I tell him that I love him and will try to do better.

A twelve-year old.

I start by thanking God for all the good things I can think of, things that come to mind quickly and that I am glad about and can be grateful for. I think about how things are going at home and at school, how I behave towards my parents, my family, and my friends and teachers at school. What do I feel about myself and my relationship with God?

How have things gone wrong? Is there anything on my mind that I am uncomfortable with at the moment?

With my parents? Do I do my share of jobs around the house willingly and without complaining, or am I selfish and watch TV or chat or play or go out with my friends instead? Do I betray my parents' trust when they are out or when I am with my friends? Do I lie about doing my homework? Do I get my brother or sister into trouble to protect myself?

With my friends? Do I speak in a horrible way or unfairly about others behind their back? Do I bully others, or take sides to stay in with the crowd? Am I jealous? Do I share my friends with others?

With others? Do I try to avoid contact with teachers because of my lack of work? Am I grateful when someone does me a favour? Do I help my Gran/other people when I am asked?

When I have tried to look at some of the ways my life has gone wrong, I tell God I am sorry. I look to see how I can change and try to understand that God wants me to be happy.

A young adult.

I think that for a lot of us the very word 'Confession' (which let's face it is still what we call it!) is enough to conjure up images of an angry God waiting for us to cower before him and tell him how horrible we are.

I know I always have to remind myself that Confession is a Sacrament: something that's meant to be there to help me, not give me a hard time, and that like the father in the Prodigal Son parable, God is waiting for us with compassion, and is ready to run out and meet us half way. What is important to him is not so much what we've done, but that we have chosen to come and be reconciled.

Note that in the parable, when the son 'confessed', the father didn't give him a hard time or even mention his past errors; in his happiness that his son had come back to him he just wanted to show him more love.

This parable always helps me realise I can be honest with God and rely on a loving response from someone who wants me to change so that I don't hurt him, myself or others.

After this, I usually find working out how I've failed to love God as I ought, or hurt or upset other people, or myself, a good starting point for my Confession.

I also find myself remembering bits from an examination of conscience sheet we used at school for class reconciliation services; probably because the questions were really relevant to life and made me think. I remember the one that stuck out for me was 'Have you said anything about one of your friends recently that you wouldn't have said if that friend were in the room?'

Some of the others were things like: do I lie? do I cheat? do I criticise people in my thoughts or words? do I try to pray? am I moody or snappy with the people I love most? do I hold grudges, or do I try to forgive in the way I ask God to forgive me? do I do anything in my life that helps other people? do I give to the poor or underprivileged? do I betray confidences?

I think most of us cringe inwardly at most of these questions, it's not hard to find things about ourselves that we're sorry for and want to change when we look at them.

In fact, it can be a bit overwhelming to realise just how many things we do that we are not proud of, and that's when I try to remember again that God is not a policeman who is after us to record our crimes, but someone who wants literally to 'absolve' us of them and give us a fresh start and the grace to change. All he wants is for us to be honest, and to honestly want to change.

There is not much point in finding some nice pat standard 'sins', reeling them off in a list and coming out again thinking 'oh good, that's over for another six months/year'. We have to want Confession to change us.

A mature adult called to the single state.

I start with thanksgiving. I begin by looking at God's invitation to me; an invitation that asks me to get closer to him, and I see that he does not take advantage of that situation; he invites but doesn't force. My preparation is a bit like playing a video of my life since my last Sacrament of Reconciliation and stopping it in various places in gratitude for God's love.

I reflect on what I'm grateful for in my everyday life. I then think of the people I live with: Am I happy with the way I relate to them? Am I open to relationships with friends/family/the people with whom I work? Do I only want to have these relationships on my own terms? Am I only prepared to relate to those whom I find easy? Are there people with whom relationships have deteriorated? What efforts am I prepared to make to rectify this? Do I express my feelings for other people in appropriate ways? Do I misuse my single state by being self-centred? Do I use it as a barrier to being open to others?

Have I been open and dealt fairly with those for whom I work? How do I treat resources that belong to my work place? Do I put my full self into my work? Am I willing to listen? Have I been open to the community where I live and work?

Have I been actively working at my relationship with God? Have I allowed that relationship to grow? What have I learnt about God recently Have I taken time for prayer — or have I just fitted it in? How conscious have I been of God's presence in my life? Do I thank God for my gifts? Have I been open to the teaching of Jesus? Does my life reflect Jesus to those around me? Have I tried to live Gospel values? Do I thank God for gifts given and received? Have I played my part fully in the community of the Church? How do I react to people who are in need? Do I live a more extravagant lifestyle than is necessary? Do I take care of my body and my health? How have I used my resources/talents?How have I used the world's resources? How am I responsible for terrorism, for poverty and exploitation in the Third World or unrest in troubled parts of the world?

I finish by asking myself how would I respond if Jesus asked me: 'When I needed a neighbour, were you there?'.

A married person.

I begin by allowing myself to become aware of the good things that have happened in my life recently and I allow myself to be filled with thanksgiving and praise. In spite of all the difficulties and failures there is always something to be grateful for.

I reflect on my relationship with my partner. I exchanged vows with my partner when I married. Does my partner still come first in the order of my priorities, or does someone or something else take first place? — for example, the children, my parents, my house, my hobby, my work? How long is it since I had a good 'heart to heart' talk with my marriage partner? Do we speak to each other about ourselves as a couple and how we are relating to one another? Are there any no-go areas in our conversations? Can we express our feelings for one another freely, negative feelings, like anger, disappointment, criticism, as well as love, knowing that they will be accepted without retaliation? Do we make time to go out together or do we feel the need always to have friends with us?

And if there are children: Do I spend enough quality time with my children? Do I listen to them, talk to them? How much time do I give? If they have heard my partner and me arguing, or being snappy with each other, have they also heard us making up, seen us being reconciled? Do I indulge all their wants and take the line of least resistance or do I discriminate? Am I honest with them? Do I really know my children, what they enjoy doing, what they think of school, who their friends are, what frightens them, what they think of me? Do my children know me? Do they see me as a friend, someone they must and can talk to? Do I encourage and praise them enough or am I always nagging? How do I bring God over to them? Is he the God of Love and a friend?

With my relatives and friends: Am I honest and sincere with them, or, do I hold back the truth from them as I see it, in case it 'spoils' our relationship? What is the level of my conversation? Is it always superficial and trivial, or sometimes profound and serious? If the occasion demands, or offers itself, do I bring God and my religion into the conversation or am I too embarrassed, or unsure of myself, to do so?

In my work: Do I do my job as well as I possible can? Do I honestly earn the wage or salary I receive? If I am in a position of authority, am I fair and just with the people who work for me? Am I trustworthy? Do I make a fair balance between work and home?

My relationship with God: How much time do I spend getting to know God? Is it just an hour a week, and that because there is some rule that says I have to? Do I ever speak about God, or prayer, or faith with my partner? Do we pray together? How often do I pray for my partner and my children? Do I encourage family prayer, for example, saying grace before meals? Do I help to create a Christian atmosphere at home? Do I encourage Christian standards, and are there Christian symbols, such as a crucifix, to remind us of the place of God in the family home? Would my friends, or the people I work with, recognise that I am different in some way because I am a Christian?

I allow myself to feel sorrow for all the disorder in my life, for my failure to love, and to let love take over. I turn to God in my sorrow.

A diocesan priest

I begin with thanksgiving, allowing myself to be aware of the positive signs of God's love and action in my ministry, and personal life. I look at what my relationship with Christ is like, in my personal prayer, in the Divine Office, in my work, in my leisure time?

How far is the *Eucharist* the centre of my life, prayer, work, and relationships?

How far do I allow my life of *celibacy* to build up my relationship with Christ and other people? Am I faithful to it as an apostolic commitment in a well thought-out way?

Am I *possessive* about anyone? Do I let people come close, but not too close? Have I got real friends? How do I treat them? Do I respect my inner space and the space of others?

Do I love the *Church*? Am I truly open to the Church's teaching? What about my spirit of obedience and faith? How do I deal with aspects of the Church's social and ethical teaching that cause me to question, to be concerned, angry, negative, fearful or depressed? How do I respond to others who may have problems of faith and obedience? Do I have a healthy and mature relationship with my Bishop as his co-worker, and, through him, with the diocese and the wider Church? If it is not as good as it should be what practical steps can I take to improve it?

Are *my living standards* those of the poor, or the middle classes? How do I respond to or identify with the poor at all levels? In what ways do I help those who suffer the consequences of poverty? Do I make time to read scripture and theology? What papers or documentation on pastoral and moral questions do I read? Do I make sure of regular time off? What prevents me? Can these obstacles be overcome? If I do take time off, how do I spend it?

Do I see a link between *overwork* and the tensions, edginess, tiredness and lack of vision that may spoil the quality of my ministry?

How do I *listen*? Especially, how do I listen and speak in the Sacrament of Reconciliation, and when people come to me for advice? Do I reflect and pray about this?

I conclude by praying: Father, teach me, heal me, strengthen me and sustain me through this reflection I have made in Your presence and with the light of Your Spirit. I want everything I am and everything I do to be in the name of Jesus Your Son, to whom I have committed and continue to commit all my life and my love, my heart and my mind, all my resources and all my desires and dreams.

I wish to love as Your Son has loved; to love the Church for which he gave his life; the world which is his gift of love, and the countless men and women to whom he restores the glorious image in which they were made, to become a new creation.

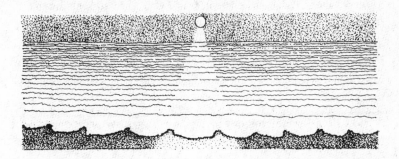

Bring together and make whole my life and ministry, my prayer and my work, my relationships and the deep longings of my heart through that pastoral charity which is Your gift and at the very centre of Your calling me to be Your priest, for the sake of Christ's Body the Church. I ask this through Jesus Christ, Your Son, and my brother, Amen.

A religious:

I establish within me an attitude of gratitude as I bring to mind particular moments recently when I've been aware of God's loving action in my life. I look at how I have responded to God's love, in the various aspects of my life as a religious.

How have I been living my life for him? Have I sought time and opportunity to be aware of his Presence? Have I created space, silence and solitude in order to hear him, see him and simply be with him?

Do I find time to read the Scriptures? Have I tried to find him in all the circumstances and events of my life? What has prevented me? Laziness? Apathy? A false sense of importance? A need to be busy? Avoidance of myself, or God?

How have I been living in his world? How do I use Creation? What is my level of awareness of greed, waste, indulgence?

How have I used my political conscience? Have I tried to inform myself on matters of importance for justice? Have I chosen to be involved by interest or action in concrete situations that come my way? Or, have I ignored them? What has prevented me? Can I bring to mind missed opportunities? Is it apathy? Fear? Embarrassment?

How have I lived my vows? Have I been aware of the call of obedience in the daily living out of what seems to be the will of God at this time or in particular events or encounters in which seeking God's will was second to my own?

How have I been living my particular *ministry*? What has been the quality of obedience within it?

Am I harbouring *resentment*? Do I seek power? Do I fail to see the value in the humdrum? Do I thwart or disbelieve in God's power to bring good out of weakness?

What is the quality of my relationships *in a celibate life*? When has chastity hurt? Who are my friends? Am I willing to share them? Am I afraid of any of these relationships for whatever reason, too intimate, too distant? Do they lead to freedom and greater loving? Or, am I demanding or selfish in my relationships? When I am with my friends is there anything which causes me to doubt, or be ashamed? What prevents me from loving? Fear? Dependency? Self-interest, anxiety for the consequences?

How do I live my *community* life? Do I enjoy being with my community, am I in harmony with those with whom I live and work or do I look for companionship elsewhere? With whom do I need to be reconciled?

In the light of my vow of *poverty* I ask myself how do I share, my time, my possessions, my own self? How much do I hanker after things? How willing am I to do without? Do I allow myself to be challenged in the way I use material things? What kind of life style do I settle for? What attachments do I have and why do I have them?

How do I spend my *leisure* time? What do I read? What do I watch on TV and for how long?

I conclude by allowing myself to be permeated with the love of God and moved to sorrow, I desire to change and to grow and I seek forgiveness and reconciliation.

A retired person:
I begin by thanking God for his unfailing love throughout my life. I celebrate all the good things that have come my way, calling to mind a few of its most recent joys.

Deep down I want to draw closer to God and ask him to show me again where I still fail to respond to him, and I ask for the grace to accept myself as I am.

How do I spend my time? Have I more time for my family, my neighbours? Do I spend more time with God in prayer; do I pray only for my own needs or do I pray for the Church and the world?

Do I accept patiently my infirmities and ailments? Do I ever thank God for my length of life and all the strengths I do have or am I pre-occupied with my limitations? Do I accept help graciously, or do I resent it? Do I make unnecessary demands on my family and friends, or do I cause them worry by my stubborn independence?

Am I given to *adverse criticism* and am I prone to judge negatively? Am I open to new ideas and am I pleased that others can do what is beyond me? Do I try to be cheerful?

Am I *preparing myself for death* in a spirit of trust and quiet confidence in God who has loved me from the beginning to now?

Prayerful reflection on Matthew 25.
In the previous chapters, we saw that reconciliation is a discovery of what it is to be loved and to love. When we realise what we have received in love, we find it easy to thank God Our Father and we understand how often we refuse the love shown to us by others.

One way of preparing for the celebration of the Sacrament of Reconciliation is to meditate on the parable of the Last Judgement (Mt 25:31-46). With the parable for guidance one can meditate on one's positive responses to others' needs, thanking God for the love one has shown. In the second series on can meditate on one's negative responses to others' needs, one's failures to show love. This helps to bring home to one the power one has to create life in someone or to destroy him/her.

When we pray this passage it will be helpful to pause after each line and meditate on incidents when we behaved well and, in the second series, behaved badly. In the first series it is as if we hear Jesus thanking us for allowing him to work through us. In the second series, it is as if we hear his sadness that we did not allow him to work through us.

You were hungry for a word of encouragement, and I praised you.
You were hungry for a greeting, and I smiled on you.
You were hungry for friendship, and I was there.

You were thirsty for acknowledgement, and I affirmed you.
You were thirsty for guidance, and I walked with you.
You were thirsty for a word of appreciation and I thanked you.

You were a stranger to love, and I welcomed you with affection.
You were a stranger to sympathy and understanding, and I listened to you.
You were a stranger to care and acceptance, and I opened my heart and took you in.

You were naked because you did not appreciate yourself, and I clothed you with confidence.
You were naked from the loss of your good name, and I stood by you.
You were stripped by betrayal, and I spoke words of support and love.

You were sick with doubt and worry, and I cheered you up and lightened your burden.
You were wounded by failure and disappointment, but I built you up and healed you.
You were in a pit of depression, and my patience gave you hope.

You were in a prison of loneliness, and through friendship I released you.
You were in a prison of guilt, and through my forgiveness I broke your chains.

You were imprisoned by the hurt and anguish of broken relationships, but I eased the pain and freed you from the memories.

'As you did this to one of the least of these brothers and sisters of mine, you did it to me.'

You were hungry for a word of encouragement, but I criticised you.
You were hungry for a greeting, but I gave you sour looks.
You were hungry for friendship, but I turned my back on you.

You were thirsty for acknowledgement, but I laughed at you.
You were thirsty for guidance, but I walked away.
You were thirsty for a word of appreciation, but I said nothing.

You were a stranger to love, but I locked you out of my heart.
You were a stranger to sympathy and understanding, and I ignored you.
You were a stranger to care and acceptance, and I gave you the cold shoulder.

You were naked because you did not appreciate yourself, and I sapped you of your confidence.
You were naked from the loss of your good name, and I spoke behind your back.
You were stripped by betrayal, and I tried to take away your dignity.

You were sick with doubt and worry, and I blamed you.
You were wounded by failure and disappointment, but I gave you the message that you were rubbish.

You were in a pit of depression, and I was impatient with you when you were struggling.

You were in a prison of loneliness, and I never invited you to join us.
You were in a prison of guilt, and I tried to destroy you.
You were imprisoned by the hurt and anguish of broken relationships, and I didn't support you.

'As I neglected to do this to one of the least of these brothers and sisters of mine, I neglected to do it to you, Jesus.'

The Sacrament of Reconciliation

If I am taking the Sacrament of Reconciliation seriously, then the time and the place for this special encounter with God are an integral part of my preparation. Perhaps, as has been mentioned, I want to confess or sing about my love for God because of a celebration in my life or because it is a special time of the year for me. Or, maybe, it is simply part of an on-going search for truth, and the will of God for me.

Just as I examine my conscience according to my age, state, and the circumstances in life, so the timing and setting will vary too. At present, usually the Sacrament takes place for most people in a Church, either in the confessional (face to face or anonymously as preferred), or perhaps as part of a penitential service. It is also possible to ask a priest for the Sacrament of Reconciliation in my home, or some other convenient and appropriate place. The most important aspect of reconciliation is my desire to draw closer to God by becoming more and more aware of how much he loves me, and by getting in touch with those areas in my life which are preventing me from responding fully to that love.

I may find it difficult to know where to begin, if I have not thought about the aspect of reconciliation in my life for quite a while. Perhaps the only time I remember confessing my sins was when I was a child. The samples given above of how I might look at the way I am living my life for God, and the response I am making, or failing to make, to his love, are offered by real people, people who see the importance of reflecting on God's love in their lives, and on the need each of us has to be reconciled with our failure to love ourselves, others and God. Each of us will have our own way of reflecting on our lives, of examining our conscience, not only according to our age and state in life, but more importantly according to who I am, and how I relate to myself, others and God. But, if I believe that my sinfulness, and failure to love affects not only me, but the community, the Body of Christ, to which I belong, then seeing forgiveness in the Sacrament of Reconciliation can be the outward sign of the healing love we all need so much.

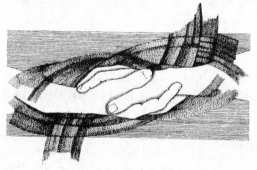

Chapter Sixteen
Reconciliation: Celebrating the Sign

The only reason that I am coming to the Sacrament of Reconciliation is to meet the God who reveals himself chiefly as prodigal of love— the forgiving lover. It brings home to me more and more that I am a sinner always needing Christ's redemption. The emphasis is on the Father's attitude towards me and my realisation of my need for him; it is not a preoccupation with my own sinfulness. My approach, therefore, to this sacrament is essentially a personal one and it will necessarily follow the particular rhythm of my personal life. It is only I who can decide when it is appropriate for me to meet God in this way, the occasions might form a pattern in my life when I follow a certain timetable or, alternatively, I may wish to receive the sacrament only at significant moments of my life during the year: a birthday, anniversary, holiday, or at the major feasts of the Church.

The reason for regular confession is to help me form an attitude which makes my gradual conversion genuine and on-going. By having to verbalise my 'refusal to love', it is brought home to me how withholding love can become a dominant force in my life. I see that, no matter how I try, I am unable to overcome this selfish tendency, and that it is only God who can change my heart to enable me to become more loving. I consciously become the poor person before God. Because the sacrament is absolutely confidential I can speak freely and honestly to the priest. If I go regularly, over a long period of time, to that same priest in the Sacrament of Reconciliation, his understanding of me and my state of life will deepen, and he will be better able to help me to grow in the love of God, myself and my neighbour. I, in turn, will know the priest who is my confessor better, and can pray for the gift of discernment for him.

Reception of this sacrament can take place in the church but may well be arranged elsewhere too. What is important is the atmosphere. Whether I am in a confessional or elsewhere, the atmosphere should be one of welcome, which the sacrament itself offers. Sometimes, I may choose a form of confession which is face to face, and at other times I may prefer to be anonymous and speak through a grille. It is important that it is easy for me to choose and that neither is imposed. Above all, I need to be at ease, confident that I will be met with the welcome of the God of Love.

Appendix: the History of Penance

All sin is an offence against God and ultimately can only be forgiven by God, but exactly what this means, and how it is to be understood and experienced, has varied significantly from century to century.

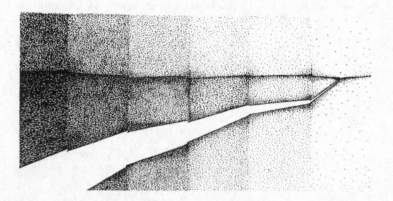

Israel's laws

Most of Israel's laws were religious, handed down from Yahweh to Moses and the other Prophets. The law was the foundation on which was built the covenant between God and his people. Sin was understood as a disruption in the relationship between God and the individual. The sinner had to perform certain actions in order to restore that relationship between a Holy God and one fallen from the holiness demanded of him. He was required, for example, to make sin offerings, to fast, to spend prolonged periods in prayer and to endure corporal punishment. The Torah, the law of Moses, revealed the will of Yahweh to his people and Jewish law was an elaborate sacramental system, although it sometimes degenerated into legalism.

Jesus was the sacrament of divine forgiveness to many of those who met him (Mk 1:15; Lk 5:18-26; Mt 18:21-22, 5:43-48), and his mission was to reconcile everyone to God. In this broad sense of a sacrament, the early Christian community was a sacrament of reconciliation for all who wanted to be saved (Jn 5:16). The only person who could not be saved was the person who refused to repent, the sinner who turned away from God or Jesus without asking for forgiveness (Jn 17:12). Because no pardon was asked, no pardon could be given. Since the Second Coming of Christ was thought to be imminent, there was no question of a second repentance and re-conversion in the early Church.

Reconciliation in the early Church

Once the Church realised that Christ was not coming in the near future the question of re-admitting sinners to the Church had to be faced. Some bishops took the hard line of refusing them permanently, but others re-admitted them. There was no formal ritual for re-admittance and it was left to the discretion of the bishop and local custom to decide the means. They were to be forgiven only once, after Baptism, because, it was believed, to fall and repent repeatedly would make a mockery of God's mercy.

Penance, from the Latin word *penitentia,* means an interior turning away from sinful attitudes and actions, a conversion of heart. Later, it came to be applied to outward acts of repentance. Eventually, in the Middle Ages, private confession was introduced and absolution from guilt and assigned works of penitence became the rule. All such works were usually referred to as penances.

Third century practice

By the third century a certain modification appeared in the ritual for public reconciliation, whereby penitents could attend Eucharistic worship until the sermon but were not permitted to receive Holy Communion. They were also allowed to perform certain works, assigned by the bishop, such as fasting, praying and giving alms. The period of their public penitence could be of short or of lasting duration and always ended with the imposition of hands by the bishop. Because of the length and severity of this public penitence, few people sought this 'second and more laborious baptism'. It tended to be availed of only after periods of persecution. Because such penitence was a sign of God's mercy and the Church granted reconciliation to the sinner, the practice was sacramental.

At this time, some bishops believed that 'a deadly sin' (e.g.. adultery, murder, idolatry) could never be forgiven by the Church. Only God could forgive such serious sins. Other bishops favoured forgiveness but demanded severe penances; imposing for example abstention from sexual intercourse in marriage, ineligibility to hold public office, exclusion from public amusements and other such stringent restrictions. On the other hand, during the 4th Century, the Church's ruling that only one opportunity of reconciliation could be offered to Christians began to soften.

Changes during the fourth century

Because bishops acted as judges in both ecclesiastical and civil courts, sin which previously had been thought of as a break in the covenant between God and the community, increasingly came to be regarded as breaking a divine law or violating an ecclesiastical law. In addition, repentance, which previously had been regarded as an act of re-conversion or change of heart leading to re-establishment of the relationship, was being looked upon as a penalty, imposed for violating the law, a payment to make amends for the offence committed against divine justice.

Penitence was a long process proceeding from the confines of remorse and guilt to the freedom of acceptance and forgiveness. Unfortunately, in practice, most Christians looked on confession as something to be avoided at all costs, because of the particular penances imposed. The great majority of Christians felt no need for public penitence and sought the remission of their sins through the earlier means of prayer and almsgiving, fasting at the appointed times and attending the Eucharist. By the close of the fifth century, the rigours of the penitential system had given rise to some notable and far reaching consequences. Bishops and priests were forbidden to become public penitents because of the disgrace it would bring upon the priesthood; the rule forbidding sexual relations after admission to the order of penitence was one of the factors that led to the rise of clerical celibacy in the West. When people were seeking to live a life of holiness, they renounced many of the same things that penitents were required to forego, marriage, wealth, public careers etc. What was formerly a self-imposed practice became a law for priests in the Roman Church.

With the disappearance of the canonical penance system, a new practice emerged, whereby people seeking to develop their spiritual lives sought guidance from a monk, usually a layman. During the course of guidance, they spoke openly about their sins so their 'spiritual father' could help them to progress in the spiritual life.

Reconciliation during the middle ages

During the 5th Century, Ireland was converted by Patrick, who introduced a liturgy which was quite different from the other forms in Christianity. One difference was that monks introduced repeated private confession and continuous works of penitence after Baptism. These same monks brought these customs to the Continent after the fall of the Roman Empire. Although they were condemned by many of the European clergy and in the Council of Toledo, 589, by 650, a similar council in Cyhalon, France, had approved them. The monks used to carry books with lists of sins and tables of appropriate penances. So, confessors were cast in the role of judges representing God as the Judge, and imposing punishment for violating God's law. There were also increasing misuses of private penitence, but it was not until the 11th century that the hierarchy succeeded in having the penitential books withdrawn from circulation.

Church authority then decided to regulate private penitence with Church laws. The Fourth Lateran Council decreed that all Catholics who committed serious sins had to confess them to a priest within a year. Thus, in 1215, the practice of private confession became an official sacrament of repentance in Western Christianity. During the period, 900-1200, penitents were reconciled immediately after confession just in case the penitent died before he had time to complete the penances required and thus be without the priest's assurance of God's forgiveness. Thus absolution was felt to apply to the sins themselves and did not necessarily involve penance.

A debate ensued about what precisely effected God's forgiveness, some regarded contrition as the effective element in confession, that in confession, sin was removed by contrition and then forgiven by God. However, others maintained that if the priest accepted the punishment for sins, he effectively forgave the sins themselves. Thomas Aquinas believed that both contrition and restitution were involved. During the debates, however, various distinctions emerged which were to be important in later theology:

The distinction between mortal and venial sin. Mortal sin required public penitence in the early Church, venial sin was less serious and therefore could be pardoned privately.

The distinction between perfect and imperfect contrition. Perfect contrition so altered a person's attitude that she/he resolved never to sin again, because she/he believed sin had no place in the heart of someone who loved God. Imperfect contrition did not necessarily change a person's behaviour but it might motivate her/him to sin less often or to avoid mortal sins.

The distinction between eternal punishment and temporal punishment. Absolution could remit the eternal punishment, which the sin had earned but not the temporal punishment. God's mercy released people from the punishment of hell, but God's justice still had to be satisfied by penances performed over a period of time. If the sinner died before the penance was completed she/he would have to undergo purification in purgatory.

Indulgences

Indulgences were introduced as a legal way of avoiding God's punishment. An indulgence was to substitute for all the penance a person had to perform for her/his confessed sins. A plenary indulgence was regarded as full payment of penalties due to sin, payment to be made either on earth or in purgatory. Ordinary indulgences came from the Church's treasury of spiritual merits accumulated by the merits of the suffering Christ and the superabundant merits of the saints. Bishops could unlock this treasury and apply indulgences to whomsoever they might deem worthy (e.g. financial contributors, pilgrims, people performing special devotions etc) but only the Pope could grant a plenary indulgence.

The Reformation

Both Luther and Calvin advocated non-obligatory confessions and maintained that the doctrine of individual sins needing absolution from a priest, was a mediaeval practice and turned the good Christian custom of confession into a form of mental torture. In consequence, in both Lutheran and Calvinistic Churches, even private confessions disappeared. In the Anglican Church, Confession was regarded as a less important sacrament than Baptism or the Eucharist, because it was regarded as a sacrament instituted by the Church and not by Christ. It was a rite to be administered to the sick and the dying but not practised in the time of health.

Council of Trent

The Catholic Church introduced some reforms but also upheld the importance of the sacrament of confession. The Reformers had tried to rid the sacrament of confession of its legal status, but the Roman Catholic Bishops, because of their traditional role as judges, resisted. The Council of Trent treated the sacrament of confession both from the point of view of theology and of Canon Law. It was deemed that, theologically, the sacrament was necessary for salvation and that, canonically, mortal sins were to be confessed within a year. As a result, confession became the usual preparation for Holy Communion, which was received once a year. It was also decided that priests were to be trained in Divine and Church Law, so as to be better able to hear confessions. From 1614, priests were obliged to hear confessions from behind a screen both in order to preserve the anonymity of the penitent and to avoid solicitation.

Vatican II

The Orthodox Churches had always regarded the penance rite at the beginning of Mass as a sacramental rite. Where private confession was concerned, which is usually the prelude to the annual reception of Holy Communion, the penitent only confessed what weighed most heavily on his mind and the priest prayed for God's mercy and forgiveness for him. The Eastern Churches never had a concept of confession as a juridical act. They always believed that sins were forgiven by God and the purpose of penitential works was not to pay a debt for breaking a law, but to grow in holiness.

In the west a new way of thinking about morality came with the emergence of biblical scholarship, which returned to the idea that it was not the law, but the covenant between God and his people, that ought to be the norm of morality. Although it could be spelt out in do's and don'ts, sin should be understood as the breaking down of a relationship of love and not the breaking of a law.

So, when laws like eating meat on Fridays or fasting before communion were relaxed, theologians wondered whether such a breaking of the law would incur eternal damnation. Again, with the rise of social awareness in the 1960s, ordinary people began to ask about the wider moral issues, such as, whether there should be equal rights for all ethnic groups, whether millions should be condemned to live in dire poverty in a land of affluence, and whether people should be slaughtered in wars. What had the Church, which had concentrated for so long on its own laws and the Ten Commandments, to say about these issues?

How did one confess social sin?

With Vatican II, Bishops reiterated the traditional Catholic theology of penance, because they had all been brought up in the way of private confession and absolution. Having learnt from Church historians how the practice of penance had changed in the past, however, they admitted it could also change in the future, but this is all they had to say on the matter.

Modern times

In 1976, three forms of rite for use in the Catholic Church, one private, one public, one communal, were substituted for the Tridentine rite of 1614. These rites stressed reconciliation, rather than confession, and the use of scripture as well as prescribed prayers. Since then, attempts have been made to update the Sacrament — penitential services and even general absolution being given during a certain period of experimentation.

Nonetheless, in spite of this, the number of people frequenting the Sacrament of Reconciliation has diminished greatly in recent years. This could be because people's sense and understanding of sin has changed.

Sadly, as we have seen many of us have little sense of sin because we have little understanding of real love.

On the other hand, many people, who attended the Sacrament in the past did so out of fear, and, even perhaps out of superstition, believing that they could not receive communion at Mass on Sunday without having been to confession beforehand. Now, many more people are coming to Mass and communion without that fear.

It must be said too, that some people's experience of confession had often been rather negative. After the preparation for First Confession there was little help available to form conscience and develop people's understanding and need of reconciliation and healing. With the development in society generally, of psychological counselling in so many areas of life, people who used to bring all their problems to the priest in confession, are, now, being offered marriage counselling, therapy, psycho-synthesis, personal growth and the like. This can be very positive for many but it would be a great pity, if it was seen as a substitute for the Sacrament of Reconciliation.

This growth could, in fact, be the basis of our realisation that this Sacrament offers the forgiveness and healing touch of a loving God. While we may experience this healing in other ways, the Sacrament is the great symbol (or outward sign) and reminds us of our membership of a community. It is the way we are publicly and formally reconciled to God and one another, through the Church's Healing Ministry, much in the same way as the Sacrament of Marriage is a public announcement that a couple are committed to each other.

There is much still to be done to bring to people's attention the positive and helpful role that the rite of Reconciliation can play in their lives. It may, in the future, as in the past, take very different forms, constantly being adapted and re-adapted to suit the changing needs in people's lives.

Services of Reconciliation

Flor McCarthy, SDB

Publisher's Note: These Services of Reconciliation, or Penitential Services, may be conducted with or without a priest/priests. When a service is celebrated in the absence of a priest, at the point where people would have made their confession and received absolution, they might reflect for a moment on their sins and make an act of contrition.

Introduction

I wish to make a few brief points by way of an introduction to these Services of Reconciliation, or Penitential Services.

The Services are modelled on those contained in the *Rite of Penance*.

We should try to create a welcoming atmosphere in the church. To this end, the lights could be dimmed and some suitable background music played as the people are assembling.

As regards music during the ceremony, at the very least there should be an opening and closing hymn sung by everyone.

While the confessions are in progress, a small choir could sing some hymns, or background music could be played, or some psalms could be recited. (Suitable psalms can be found in the aforementioned *Rite of Penance*). However, care should be taken to allow time for silent prayer and reflection.

Needless to say, the more priests that are available the better. That way the ceremony can be paced nicely, and more time given to each penitent, without prolonging it unduly.

The people should be encouraged to stay until the end of the ceremony. And wherever possible involve lay people in the ceremony.

Of the six services which follow, two are for use at Christmas, and two for use near or during Holy Week. The other two can be used at any other time of the year.

Finally, additional material for the examination of conscience will be found in Chapter Fifteen of Fr McGowan's book.

Flor McCarthy

Service of Reconciliation:
Hymn to Love

Greeting and Introduction

In the name of the Father ...
Grace, mercy and peace be with you from God the Father and Jesus
Christ, our Saviour.

Jesus says, 'By *this* everyone will know that you are my disciples.'
He wasn't talking about learning, hard work, distinctive dress, lifestyle, titles ... He was talking about love: 'Everyone will know that you
are my disciples *by the love you have for one another.'*

Love is the heart of the Gospel. In this ceremony we will examine
ourselves on love. Failure to live by this command of Christ is not only
the worst sin, but in a sense, the only sin for a Christian. [Pause]

Opening prayer

Almighty and ever-lasting God, your love for us surpasses all that
we ask or deserve. Open for us the treasures of your mercy. Forgive
all that weighs on our conscience, and grant us more even than we dare
to ask. We make this prayer through Christ our Lord.

Scripture Reading

(What follows is from St Paul's famous hymn to love: I Cor. 13:1-
7. If love is to become visible and tangible it has to take flesh in a
person. The reading is adapted so that it talks, not about love in the
abstract, but about a loving person. And the reading is combined with
the reflection on our lives. Use two voices; one for the scriptural part
(in italics), the other for the reflection on it).

I may speak all the languages of earth and heaven, but if I have no love in my heart, I am just a gong booming or a cymbal clashing.

I could be the greatest orator that ever was, or the greatest preacher, but if I'm not a loving person, it's all so much noise. Words can never take the place of deeds.

I may have the gift of prophecy and the knowledge of every hidden truth; if I have no love in my heart, I am nothing.

It doesn't matter how much I know, or how many letters I have after my name, if I'm not a loving person, it will count for nothing.

I may have faith strong enough to move mountains; but if I have no love in my heart, I am nothing.

Faith isn't everything. In fact, a loveless faith is worthless. It is like a fruit tree that doesn't produce fruit.

I may give all I possess to the needy, I may give my body to be burnt, but if I have no love in my heart, it will do me no good whatever.

Sacrifice is a great and praiseworthy thing. But it has to be motivated by love. Otherwise it will be of no spiritual benefit to us.

A loving person is patient.

To be patient is to be calm, uncomplaining, self-controlled ...

A loving person is kind.

To be kind is to be obliging, thoughtful, helpful, considerate, gentle, warm-hearted ...

A loving person envies no one.

The envious person longs for the possessions, the gifts, or the achievements of others. The loving person on the other hand is grateful for the gifts God has given to him/her, and tries to develop and use them fully.

A loving person is never boastful.

The boastful person shows off, brags, and craves recognition. The loving person keeps a low profile.

A loving person is never conceited.
To be conceited is to be vain, proud, arrogant, domineering ...
The loving person is humble, modest, self-effacing ...

A loving person is never rude.
To be rude is to be bad-mannered, discourteous, abusive ...
The loving person is always courtous, gracious, friendly ...

A loving person is never selfish.
A selfish person is greedy, mean, self-centered ..
A loving person is generous, unselfish, thinks of others ..

A loving person is not quick to take offence.
The loving person is not touchy, over-sensitive, but is calm, serene, good-tempered .

A loving person keeps no score of wrongs.
The loving person will forgive you when you wrong him/her, and won't hold it against you.
The unloving person won't forgive you, but will bear a grudge against you, and refuse you courtesy and kindness.

A loving person takes no pleasure in the sins of others.
A loving person is not always harping on the faults of others , or always criticising them, and passing judgement on them ...

A loving person delights in the truth.
A loving person concentrates on the good in others, praising and affirming them, and rejoicing in their achievements.

There is nothing a loving person cannot face.
Far from being weak or soft, a loving person is tough and is not easily put off.

There is no limit to the faith of a loving person.
A loving person is prepared to think and believe the best about people.

There is no limit to the hope of a loving person.

A loving person never gives up on anyone or on any situation.

There is no limit to what a loving person is prepared to endure.

A loving person will face hardship, sacrifice, even insults without opting out. A loving person stays the course.

Litany of sin

My brothers and sisters, let us ask pardon for our failings.

R. Lord, have mercy.

For limiting our love to words. R.

For being impatient with others. R.

For being irritable, and lacking in self-control. R.

For being intolerant towards others. R.

For being unkind in thought, word, or deed. R.

For being envious or jealous of others. R.

For being boastful. R.

For being proud and arrogant. R.

For being rude and discourteous towards others. R.

For being selfish. R.

For failing to help. R.

For taking offence easily. R.

For bearing a grudge and harbouring ill-feelings towards others. R.

For failing to apologise when we were wrong. R.

For failing to ask for forgiveness when we hurt someone. R.

For refusing to forgive when we were hurt. R.

For being criticial of others. R.

For being judgemental. R.

For failing to encourage and affirm others. R.

For being selective in our love. R.

For not having shown sufficient trust in others. R.

For having little hope for someone. R.

For the times our love has been fickle and short-lived. R.

For failing to trust in God's unconditional love for us.

For failing to return God's love.

For failing to appreciate and return the love of others. R.

For failing to love ourselves with a wholesome love. R.

For failing to take care of our environment. R.

I confess to almighty God ...

Let us now join in the prayer that Jesus taught us, asking God to forgive us as we forgive others.

Our Father ...

(The priests go to the places assigned for confession. The penitents who desire to confess their sins go to the priest of their choice. When the service is celebrated without a priest, participants might reflect on their need for pardon and make an act of contrition.)

Prayers after confession / reflection on our need for pardon.

It's the heart that matters. The heart is what I am, deep down. It is the real me. We have to ask God to heal the wounds of the hearts so that we may bear the fruits of love.

R. Lord, hear our prayer.

Lord, open our hearts when they are closed. R.

Warm them when they are cold. R.

Soften them when they are hard. R.

Brighten them when they are in darkness. R.

Ligthen them when they are weighed down with worry. R.

Fill them when they are empty. R.

Calm them when they are troubled and afraid. R.

Cleanse them when they are sullied. R.

Heal them when they are wounded. R.

Mend them when they are broken. R.

Concluding prayer of thanksgiving

Lord, we thank you for the goodness you have shown us in forgiving our sins. May we who have experienced your loving kindness be generous in forgiving others. We ask this through Christ our Lord.

Blessing and Dismissal

The Lord is a faithful sentinel who never sleeps and who guards his people night and day.
R. Amen.

May the Lord guide you in the way of his love, and fill your with Christlike patience.
May he give you the strength to walk in newness of life and to please him in all things.

Go in the grace and peace of the Lord who frees us from our sins.
R. Thanks be to God.

Service of Reconciliation:
The Pharisee and the Tax Collector

Greeting and Introduction
In the name of the Father ...
Grace, mercy and peace be with you from God the Father, and Jesus
Christ our Saviour.

Jesus told a story about two people who went into the temple to pray.
Only one of them returned home at rights with God. That was the one
who humbly confessed his sins.
We have an opportunity this evening/morning to imitate him. If we do,
then we will go home at peace with God. [Pause]

Opening prayer
Lord, enlighten us so that we may be able to see our sins; give us
the courage to accept responsibility for them, the humility to confess
them truthfully, and the confidence that you will forgive them. We
make this prayer through Christ our Lord.

Scripture Reading (Luke 18: 9-14)

Jesus spoke the following parable to some people who prided
themselves on being virtuous and despised everyone else.

'Two men went up to the Temple to pray. One of them was a
Pharisee, the other a tax collector. The Pharisee stood there and made
this prayer to himself: "I thank you, God, that I am not grasping,
unjust, and adulterous like the rest of mankind, and particularly that
I am not like this tax collector here. I fast twice a week; I pay tithes on
all I have." And he went on praying in that manner.

The tax collector stood some distance away, not daring even to raise his eyes to heaven. He simply beat his breast and said, "God, be merciful to me, for I am a sinner.'

I tell you that the tax collector went home at rights with God, whereas the Pharisee did not. For everyone who exalts himself will be humbled, and everyone who humbles himself will be exalted.'

Reflecting on the Scripture Reading

Where did the Pharisee go wrong? Firstly, his attitude to God was all wrong. He felt no need to ask God for anything, certainly not forgiveness for sin. On the contrary, it was God who owed something to him — a reward for the good deeds he had done. We can never put God in our debt.

Secondly, his attitude towards himself was wrong. He prided himself on his own supposed goodness. He confessed sins all right (greed, injustice, adultery), but they were not his own sins. They were the sins of others. It's easy to get into the habit of confessing the sins of others. But it's dangerous because it prevents us from looking at our own sins. The Pharisee did have sins. He was arrogant, proud, self-righteous, smug, judgmental.

And finally his attitude towards others was completely wrong. He despised them. As a result, he was harsh and unfair in the way he judged them.

And where did the Tax Collector go right? He concentrated on himself, and left the sins of others between them and God. With radical humility and honesty he laid bare his heart before God, saying, *'Lord be merciful to me for I am a sinner.'*

The sacrament of reconciliation is not an opportunity for measuring ourselves against others, or for confessing their sins. It is an opportunity for confessing our own sins. To admit our failures is the first step towards doing something about them.

Many approach confession with a prepared list of sins. The things on that list are usually trivial matters, and don't vary much from one confession to the next.

It would have been easy for the Tax Collector to produce a list of sins. But he didn't do this. He did something better. He said, 'I am a sinful man.'

Not that a list is a bad thing in itself. We should confess what we consider our most serious sins. But let us be aware of what they are — symptoms of a deeper malaise.

What if we can't come up with any specific sins? We can still say in all truth, 'I am a sinner.' We are sinful, fallen people - that is the reality. Sin is not just an act or series of acts, but *a condition* in which we live. That is the great truth which the Tax Collector grasped. One of the great problems of our time is people's failure to know themselves, to recognise evil and deal with it within themselves.

Litany of sin.

The Pharisee didn't do anything wrong. It was his attitudes that were wrong. Attitudes are vital, but are seldom considered as sinful.
R. Lord, be merciful to me a sinner.

For the times we have been guilty of sinful attitudes. R.

For the times we have failed to acknowledge that we owe everything to God. R.

For failing to give God thanks for whatever good we have been able to do. R.

For failing to have recourse to God in humble, heart-felt prayer. R.

For the times we have worshipped God with our lips while our hearts were far from him. R.

For the times we have stood before God in pride and presumption. R.

For the times we have been complacent in the assumption of our own goodness and virtue. R.

For our failure to recognise and look at our dark side. R.

For the times we have been blind to our own sins, even serious ones. R.

For the times we have been quick to draw attention to the sins of others, even trivial ones. R.

For the times we have looked down on others. R.

For the times we have been harsh and unfair in judging others. R.

For the times when, like the Pharisee, we have concentrated on appearances, rather than on trying to be authentic persons before God. R.

For failing to practise what we preach. R.

For seeking our own honour and glory in everything. R.

For spoiling the good we do by bragging about it. R.

For the sins we commit which we are not even aware of. R.

[Pause]

Confiteor

My brothers and sisters, let us call to mind the goodness of God, and acknowledge our sins, so that we may receive his merciful forgiveness.

I confess to almighty God ...

Let us join in the prayer that Jesus taught us, asking God to forgive us as we forgive others.

Our Father ...

(The priests go to the places assigned for confession. The penitents who desire to confess their sins go to the priests of their choice. When the service is celebrated without a priest, participants might reflect on their need for pardon and make an act of contrition.)

Prayers after confession / reflection on our need for pardon.

The most important thing about each of us is our capacity for goodness. We have hands that can care, eyes that can see, ears that can hear, tongues that can speak, feet that can walk, and above all hearts that can love. Let us pray together:

Lord, make me an instrument of your peace.

Where there is hatred, let me sow love.

Where there is injury, pardon.

Where there is doubt, faith.

Where there is darkness, light.

Where there is sadness, joy.

O Divine Master, grant that I may

not so much seek to be consoled, as to console;

to be understood as to understand;

to be loved as to love.

For it is in giving that we receive;

it is in pardoning that we are pardoned;

it is in dying that we are born to eternal life.

Concluding prayer of thankgiving

Lord, we thank you for your goodness to us. You have shown your love for us by forgiving our sins. May we who have experienced your loving kindness be generous in forgiving others. We ask this through Christ our Lord.

Blessing and Dismissal

The Lord is a faithful sentinel who never sleeps and who guards his people night and day.

R. Amen.

May the Lord guard you from all evil.

May he never allow you to stumble or fall.

May he surround you with his favour as with a shield.

Go in the grace and peace of the Lord who frees us from our sins.
R. Thanks be to God.

A Service of Reconciliation
Holy Week, One

Place a number of small crucifixes around the church. Put a votive lamp and a small cloth beside each.

Greeting and Introduction

In the name of the Father ...
Grace, mercy and peace be with you from God the Father and Jesus Christ, our Saviour.

The day Christ died is not called 'Bad Friday' but 'Good Friday'. What makes it good is the love of Christ. He loved us to the point of dying for us.

The people who put him to death were not a uniquely evil group of people, acting from the vilest possible motives. They belonged to the same human family as you and I. This may be a troubling kinship but we cannot reject it. Dark evil sleeps in us all.

The Passion of Jesus helps us to confront the evil within us. It also helps us to deal with pain, rejection, failure, death. [Pause]

Opening prayer
All-powerful God, by the suffering and death of your Son, may we receive forgiveness for our sins, and strength and protection in our weakness. We ask this through Christ our Lord.

Reflecting on the Passion Story

(Note: Here the reading and the reflection on our lives are combined. Use two voices; one for the scriptural part (in italics), the other for the reflection on it. The aim is to try to break the mould regarding the way people look at sin, and persuade them to look deeper).

As they came in sight of Jerusalem, tears came into his eyes and he said, 'Jerusalem, Jerusalem! I longed to gather your children to myself, as a hen gathers her chickens under her wings, but you refused. The day is coming when your enemies will encircle you. They will destroy you and all your children within you. Yet all this could have been avoided if only you had grasped the opportunity for peace that God gave you.'

What tears Jesus might shed over the many wars and conflicts that plague the world today. Yet the opportunities for peace are there too, but how few grasp them.

In our own lives we know conflicts too. How much pain they cause and harm they do. Yet how slow we are to try to resolve them. [Pause]
R. *Father, forgive us, we know not what we do.*

They took the colt, and Jesus sat on it. Many people spread their cloaks on the road, others cut branches from the trees and spread them in his path. And they were all shouting, 'Hosanna to the Son of David! Blessings on him who comes in the name of the Lord.'

Jesus' disciples showed their loyalty to him in the teeth of bitter opposition from the Pharisees.

It's easy to witness to Christ in church. Not so easy out in an indifferent and sometimes hostile world. But that is precisely where the witness is needed, and where we often fail. [Pause]
R. *Father, forgive us, we know not what we do.*

While they were at supper Jesus said, 'Tonight you will all lose faith in me.' But Peter said, 'Even if all the others should lose faith in you,

I will never lose faith in you. I'm ready to go to prison, even to die with you.'

Brave words. Peter thought he was brave and strong. How little he knew about himself. When the crunch came he denied Jesus.

What are my words worth? My affirmations of loyalty, my professions of faith, my promises. How well do I know myself? Am I aware of my weak side? [Pause]
R. *Father, forgive us, we know not what we do.*

While at supper, Jesus was troubled in spirit and declared, 'I tell you most solemnly, one of you will betray me.' On hearing this, Judas got up and left the room. It was night outside.

Jesus was deeply hurt at the thought of being betrayed by one of his own. The treachery of a friend is much more hurtful than the treachery of an enemy.

To betray Christ is to leave the light and pass into darkness. But to betray anyone is the same thing. At times we all betray our ideals, if not our friends. [Pause]
R. *Father, forgive us, we know not what we do.*

When they came to the garden, Jesus took Peter, James and John with him. And a sudden fear came over him, and great distress.

And he said to them, 'My soul is ready to die with sorrow. Stay awake and watch with me.'

Jesus was sorrowful, lonely, and fearful at the realisation of the terrible death that was imminent. He was in desperate need of some human warmth and closeness. So he turned to the three disciples, but found them sleeping. They left him to drink the cup of sorrow alone. How many times I have been blind to, or worse, indifferent to, the pain of someone close to me - a neighbour, a workmate, even a member of my own family? [Pause]
R. *Father, forgive us, we know not what we do.*

They took Jesus to the house of Caiphas, the high priest, where the scribes and elders were assembled. They were looking for evidence, however false, so that they could pass the death sentence on him.

The people who plotted Jesus' death were religious people.   Religion sometimes brings out the worst in people, making them narrower, more bigoted, and more apt to hate and kill.

But religion can also bring out the best in people. True religion liberates the heart and the mind, and fosters harmonious relationships with others. What does it bring out in me? [Pause]
R. *Father, forgive us, we know not what we do.*

Anxious to placate the crowd, Pilate released Barabbas. Then, having ordered Jesus to be scourged, he handed him over to be crucified.

Pilate knew that Jesus was innocent, but he yielded to pressure. He was thinking about his job.

We think of the wrongs done and the injustices perpetrated in our times for financial or political gain. [Pause]
R. *Father, forgive us, we know not what we do.*

After scourging Jesus, the soldiers dressed him up in purple, twisted some thorns into a crown and put it on him. And they saluted him, 'Hail, king of the Jews!' They struck him with a reed and spat on him.

To have someone in our power, and to oppress, to take advantage of, to inflict pain on, or humiliate that person, particularly when the victim is incapable of defending himself/herself. [Pause]
R. *Father, forgive us, we know not what we do.*

As they were leading him away they seized a man, Simon from Cyrene, who was coming in from the country, and made him shoulder the cross and carry it behind Jesus.

Simon was not a volunteer; he was a conscript. We don't find it easy to carry the burden of another. We think we have enough burdens of our own. [Pause]

R. *Father, forgive us, we know not what we do.*

One of the thieves abused Jesus, but was rebuked for this by the other: 'Have you no fear of God? We are getting what we deserve, but this man has done nothing wrong' Then turning to Jesus he said, 'Remember me when you come into your kingdom.' And Jesus said, 'I promise you, this day you will be with me in paradise.'

The first thief frightens us. Even with death staring him in the face, he shows no remorse for the evil he had done.

But the second thief evokes our admiration. Regarding the evil he had done he says, 'I am responsible. I am guilty.' What a refreshing attitude. Today it is common to blame someone else.

The thief's humble confession won him not only forgiveness but heaven too. [Pause]

R. *Father, forgive us, we know not what we do.*

When they reached the placed called The Skull, they crucified him there and the two criminals also. Jesus said, 'Father, forgive them; they know not what they do.'

This week each year we stand at the foot of the cross, and listen with reverence as Jesus prays for his killers. But then we return to our homes to resume our deep-rooted spites and the burden of things we won't forgive. [Pause]

R. *Father, forgive us, we know not what we do.*

'Near the cross of Jesus stood his mother, Mary the wife of Clopas, Mary of Magdala, and John the beloved disciple.'

A faithful few stayed with him to the end, even though there was nothing they could do for him. Their only ministry — that of simple presence. But a reassuring, supportive presence can mean the world to the sufferer. Faithfulness is one of the most beautiful things in the

world, but how costly it can be. [Pause]
R. Father, forgive us, we know not what we do.

About the sixth hour, darkness came over the whole land until the ninth hour. Then Jesus cried out in a loud voice, 'Father, into your hands I commend my spirit.' With these words he breathed his last.

One dies as one has lived. One doesn't suddenly become a hero or a saint in death. Having shown us how to live, Jesus showed us how to die. Death is the ultimate act of trust in and abandonment to God. But it can only grow out of a relationship with God that has been there all along, and that has been nourished by prayer. [Pause]
R. Father, forgive us, we know not what we do.

In examining our consciences, let us try to go beyond things such as distractions during prayers, impatience with the children, and so on. These are not the kind of things that put Christ to death. We need to look deeper. The questions we might ask ourselves are: Where am I in the Passion Story? And with what characters or situations can I identify? [Pause]

Confiteor

My brothers and sisters, let us call to mind the goodness of God, and acknowledge our sins, so that we may receive his merciful forgiveness.
I confess to almighty God ...

Let us join in the prayer that Jesus taught us, asking God to forgive us as we forgive others.
Our Father ...

(The priests go to the places assigned for confession. The penitents who desire to confess their sins go to the priest of their choice. When the service is celebrated without a priest, participants might reflect on their need for pardon and make an act of contrition. Afterwards they could go and reverence one of the crucifixes as a way of expressing their repentance).

Prayers after confession / reflection on our need for pardon

On this week when Christ died for sinners, let us pray to him for our own needs and the needs of others.
R. Lord, hear our prayer.

Guide the minds and hearts of governments and rulers. R.

Give courage, strength and hope to all who suffer. R.

Grant that our sufferings may teach us to be compassionate towards other sufferers. R.

Keep us faithful to God's will in the darkness of our lives. R.

That we may not be afraid to show our loyalty to you in front of unbelievers and cynics.

Help us love one another as you have loved us. R.

Gather all God's scattered children into the kingdom of salvation. R.

Grant your mercy to those who have persecuted or injured us. R.

Deliver us from the fear of death. R.

Share with the dead the glory of your resurrection. R.

Prayer of thanksgiving

God of love and mercy, we thank you for the goodness you have shown us in forgiving our sins. May we who have experienced your loving kindness be generous in forgiving others. We ask this through Christ our Lord.

Blessing and Dismissal *R. Amen.*

May the Lord help you to bear suffering with patience.

May he help you to be compassionate towards those in need or in trouble.

May his Spirit help you to be a courageous disciple of his in the world.

Go in the grace and peace of the Lord who frees us from our sins.

R. Thanks be to God.

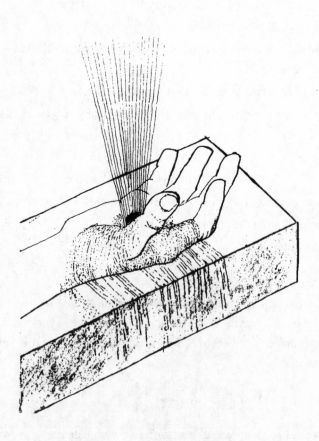

Service of Reconciliation
Holy Week, Two

Greeting and Introduction

In the name of the Father ...

Grace and peace be with you from God the Father and the Lord Jesus Christ who laid down his life for our sins.

Among the words that ring out from the liturgy of this week are the words Jesus used when he prayed for his killers: 'Father, forgive them, they know not what they do.'

Jesus pleads with the Father on our behalf. The whole purpose of his death is to reconcile us with the Father, and to help us overcome sin, evil and death. [Pause]

Opening prayer

Father, look upon our weakness and reach out to help us with your loving power. May the confession of our sins bring us the blessing of your forgiveness, and prepare us for the coming feast of our redemption. We make this prayer through Christ our Lord.

Scripture Readings

Isaiah 53:1-12 (Shortened).

See my servant. Like a sapling he grew up among us, like a root in arid ground. He appeared to have no beauty at all. He was despised and rejected by people, a man of sorrows who was well acquainted with suffering.

And yet it was our sufferings that he bore; it was our sorrows that he carried. But we couldn't see this. We thought he was being punished by God for his own sins. Whereas he was pierced for our faults, and crushed for our sins.

Through his punishment he brings us peace, and through his wounds we are healed. For we had all gone astray like sheep, each taking his own way, and the Lord burdened him with the sins of all of us.

Though he was harshly treated, he bore it humbly, never opening his mouth to complain. Nor was there anyone to plead his cause. They gave him a grave with the wicked, even though he had done no wrong. He took our sins on himself, and through his sufferings he has won pardon for all of us.

This is the word of the Lord.

Responsorial Psalm   Ps 129(130)

Response:
   Out of the depths I cry to you, O Lord.
   Lord, hear my voice.

Out of the depths I cry to you, O Lord,
Lord, hear my voice.
O let your ears be attentive
to the voice of my pleading. R.

If you, O Lord, should mark our guilt,
Lord, who would survive?
But with you is found forgiveness:
for this we revere you. R.

My soul is waiting for the Lord,
I count on his word.
My soul is longing for the Lord
more than watchman for daybreak. R.

Because with the Lord there is mercy
and fullness of redemption,
Israel indeed he will redeem
from all its iniquity. R.

Gospel: Luke 23:33-43

They crucified Jesus and the two criminals, one on the right, and the other on the left. Jesus said, 'Father, forgive them, for they know not what they do.'

The leaders jeered him: 'He saved others, let him now save himself.' The soldiers mocked him: 'If you are the king of the Jews, save yourself.' And one of the criminals hanging there abused him:

'If you are the Christ, then save yourself and us as well.'

But the other rebuked his companion, saying, 'We're getting what we deserve, but this man has done nothing wrong.' Then turning to Jesus he said, 'Lord, remember me when you come into your kingdom.' And Jesus said, 'This day you will be with me in paradise.'

This is the gospel of the Lord.

Reflecting on the Scripture Readings

Jesus is that servant Isaiah was talking about. He bore our sufferings and sorrows. He was pierced for our faults, and crushed for our sins. Though he was harshly treated, he bore it all humbly and without complaining. There was no one there to put in a word for him except one of the men who was condemned with him.

It was for us that he did all this. He took our sins on himself, and through his sufferings he has won pardon for all of us. Through his punishment he brings us peace, and through his wounds we are healed.

And yet, in order to avail of what Jesus did for us, something is required of us, as we see from the story of the two thieves.

The first thief scares us. Even with death staring him in the face, he shows no remorse for the evil he has done. Hence, he dies in his sins.

But the second thief evokes our admiration. He accepts responsibility for the evil he has done. He says, 'I am responsible. I am
guilty.' Today it is common to blame someone else. But his confession would have availed him nothing if there was no one there to help
him. But Jesus, the friend of sinners, was there. The thief's humble
confession won him not only forgiveness but heaven too. He shows
us that a clean, humble confession goes straight to the heart of God.

Jesus never retaliated. He showed us that the only way to over
come evil is through good. The sheer goodness of Jesus shines out
from every page of the Gospel. That goodness evoked goodness in
others, and will surely evoke goodness in us too. [Pause]

Reflecting on our lives
R. Lord, remember me, for I am a sinner.

What place has God in my life?
Am I a person of prayer?
Am I faithful to Sunday worship? R.

Have I contributed to the well-being and happiness of the rest of the
family by patience and genuine love?
Have I shown obedience and respect for my parents, trying to help
them in their responsibilities? R.

Have I shown myself a true parent to my children?
Have I shown myself a true and faithful husband or wife? R.

Have I a genuine concern for my neighbours?
Or do I use them, or do to them what I would not want done to me?
R.

Do I do my best to help victims of oppression, misfortune, and
poverty?
Do I share in the apostolic and charitable works of my parish? R.

Am I concerned for the good of the community in which I live?
Do I share in the work of promoting justice, morality, harmony, and
love in human relations? R.

Have I done my duty as a citizen?
Have I paid my taxes?
Have I obeyed legitimate authority? R.

In my work or profession, am I just, hard-working, and honest?
Have I been faithful to my promises and commitments? R.

If I'm in a position of responsibility or authority, do I use this for
my own advantage, or for the good of others, in a spirit of service?
Have I paid a fair wage to my employees? R.

Have I been truthful and fair, or have I injured others by deceit,
calumny, detraction, rash judgement?
Have I done violence to others by damage to life or limb, reputation
or honour?
Have I stolen or damaged the property of others? R.

Have I kept up hatred for others?
Am I estranged from others through quarrels, enmity, anger?
Do I harbour hatred and the desire for revenge?
Have I returned evil for evil? R.

Have I shown respect for myself? Or have I endangered myself
through the abuse or drink, or drugs, or my sexual powers? R.

Am I willing to accept responsibility for my sins? R.
[Pause]

Confiteor

My brothers and sisters, let us call to mind the goodness of God, and
acknowledge our sins, so that we may receive his merciful forgiveness.
I confess to almighty God ...

Let us join in the prayer that Jesus taught us, asking God to forgive us as we forgive others.

Our Father ...

(The priests go to the places assigned for confession. The penitents who desire to confess their sins go to the priest of their choice. When the service is celebrated without a priest, participants might reflect on their need for pardon and make an act of contrition. Afterwards they could go and reverence one of the crucifixes as a way of expressing their repentance).

Prayers after confession / reflection on our need for pardon

All of us are wounded by sin. Let us pray for healing.
R. Lord, graciously hear us.

For healing for the wounds caused by own sins and the sins of others. Lord, hear us. *R. Lord, graciously hear us.*

For the grace to be able to forgive those who have sinned against us, and to cast out all bitterness.
For those who are burdened with grief, or illness, or worry.
For the healing of relationships that are difficult or that have gone wrong.
For the grace to be able to overcome temptation. Lord, hear us. *R. Lord, graciously hear us.*
Let us make some practical resolution to improve our lives. [Pause]. For the grace to carry it out.

Prayer of thanksgiving

Merciful Father, we thank you for your goodness to us. Help us to rise above our human weakness, and fill our hearts with love through the death and resurrection of your Son. We ask this through Christ our Lord.

Blessing and Dismissal

R. Amen.

May Christ, the Good Shepherd, guide you along the right path.

May he give you a sense of his comforting presence when you walk through the valley of darkness.

May he enable you to forgive those who sin against you and overcome evil through goodness.

Go in the grace and peace of the Lord who frees us from our sins.

R. Thanks be to God.

Albert Carpentier, OP

Services of Reconciliation
Christmas, One

THEME: CHRIST, THE LIGHT OF THE WORL.

HAVE SMALL VOTIVE CANDLES AVAILABLE TO THE PEOPLE.

Greeting and Introduction

In the name of the Father ...

The grace and peace of God our Father and the Lord Jesus Christ be with you.

We are gathered to prepare ourselves to celebrate the birth of Jesus. We begin by lighting the candles on our Advent wreath. (A server lights the candles).

At this, the darkest time of the year, the Church lights candles to remind us that Christ is the light of the world, a light no darkness can overpower. Let us open our hearts this evening so that the light of Christ may enter and banish every kind of darkness. [Pause]

Opening prayer

Almighty God, from whom all light comes, look with compassion on us who live in darkness and in the shadow of death. May the coming of your only Son dispel the darkness of our sins and help us to live as children of light. We ask this through the same Christ our Lord.

Scripture Reading (*All of these extracts relate to the theme of light*).

Jesus says to us:

'I am the light of the world; anyone who follows me will never walk in darkness, but will always have the light of life.

Though the light has come into the world, people have shown they prefer darkness to the light because their deeds were evil ... but whoever does the truth comes out into the light, so that what they are doing is plainly seen as done in God.

You are the light of the world. No one lights a lamp to put it under a tub; they put it on a lamp-stand where it shines for everyone in the house. In the same way your light must shine in people's sight, so that seeing your good works, they may give praise to your Father in heaven.'

St John says to us:

'Anyone who claims to be in the light but hates his brother or sister is still in the dark. But anyone who loves his brother and sister is living in the light, and need not be afraid of stumbling; unlike the person who hates his brother or sister and is in the darkness, not knowing where he is going, because it is too dark to see.'

St Paul says to us:

'We are children of light and children of the day; we do not belong to the night or to darkness. God has called us out of darkness into his own wonderful light. Be like children of the light; the effects of the light are seen in complete goodness, right living and truth.'

Reflecting on the Scripture Reading

Jesus shed light through *his teaching*.

He said, 'Love your enemies, and pray for those who persecute you.' Thus he rejected the darkness of revenge, and brought the light of forgiveness and reconciliation.

In his parable of the good Samaritan he rejected the darkness of indifference, and urged people to care for one another.

In his teaching on authority he rejected the darkness of oppression, and urged those in authority not to lord it over others, but to serve them in gentleness and humility.

But it is in *his deeds* that his luminous goodness is most apparent. Countless people came to him in various kinds of darkness and went away bathed in light.

He caused the light of God's glory to shine on the lowly shepherds at his birth.

He brought sinners out of the darkness of sin into the light of God's grace and love.

He brought outcasts out of the darkness of rejection into the light of acceptance by the community.

He brought the sick and the wounded out of the darkness of illness and pain into the light of well-being.

He brought Zacchaeus out of the darkness of greed and selfishness into the light and joy of sharing.

He brought Martha and Mary out of the darkness of grief into the light of hope and life.

He brought the good thief out of the darkness of crime and hopelessness into the light of heaven itself.

He rekindled the light of faith for his doubting disciple, Thomas.

By rising from the dead he dispelled the darkness of death for all who believe in him.

Christ is truly the light of their lives, and the light of the world.

Nevertheless, there still are many people who live in darkness.

Each of us has areas of darkness in our lives. Our society has its dark areas. Let us look at some of the kinds of darkness that affect us and our society.

Litany of sin

R. Lord have mercy.
There is much darkness in our world.
For the darkness of idolatry. R.
For the darkness of war. R.
For the darkness of sectarianism. R.
For the darkness of famine. R.
For the darkness of injustice. R.
For the darkness of exploitation. R.
For the darkness of crime. R.
For the darkness of violence. R.

For the darkness of alcoholism and drug addiction. R.

For the darkness of road deaths. R.

For the darkness of abortion. R.

For the darkness of indifference. R.

For the darkness of broken relationships. R.

For the darkness of adultery. R.

For the darkness of greed. R.

For the darkness of scandal. R.

For the darkness of selfishness. R.

For the darkness of laziness and cowardice. R.

For the darkness of dishonesty. R.

For the damage done to our environment. R.

The darkness we cause to others:

By being bad-tempered towards them. R.

By passing unfair judgements on them. R.

By being critical of them. R.

By breaking our promises to them. R.

By being dishonest in our dealings with them. R.

By oppressing them. R.

By neglecting to help them. R.

By refusing to forgive them. R.

By refusing to show them friendship. R.

By failing to give them recognition. R.

By failing to show them gratitude. R.

For failing to nourish our spiritual lives through prayer. R.

For failing to play our part as members of the Christian community.
R.

Finally, for all those who have brought darkness to us. R.

[Pause]

Confiteor

My brothers and sisters, let us call to mind the goodness of God, and acknowledge our sins, so that we may receive his merciful forgiveness.

I confess to almighty God ...

Let us join in the prayer that Jesus taught us, asking God to forgive us as we forgive others.

Our Father ...

(The priests go to the places assigned for confession. The penitents who desire to confess their sins go to the priest of their choice. When the service is celebrated without a priest, participants might reflect on their need for pardon and make an act of contrition. Afterwards they might light a candle to signify their willingness to be a source of light in the world).

Prayers after confession / reflection on our need for pardon
The most important thing about each of us is our capacity for goodness. We can be a source of light. Unfortunately, through laziness or selfishness or cowardice, our light is dimmed, and we become shadows of the people we could be. Let us ask the Lord to help us through his coming.

R. Come, Lord Jesus.

Come into our weakness. R.

Come into our fears. R.

Come into our failures. R.

Come into our grieving. R.

Come into our loneliness. R.

Come into our darkness. R.

Come into our doubting. R.

Come into our despair. R.

Come into our searching. R.

Come into our poverty of heart. R.

Come into our dying. R.

Prayer of thanksgiving

God of love and mercy, we thank you for rescuing us from the kingdom of darkness and transferring us to the kingdom of your beloved Son. Help us to walk always as children of the light. We ask this through Christ our Lord.

Blessing and Dismissal

God has called us out of darkness into the wonderful light of his Son. We must try to live as children of the light. The effects of the light are seen in goodness, right living, and truth.

R. Amen.

May the Lord at his coming find your minds alight with faith.
May he find your souls alight with hope.
And may he find your hearts alight with love.

Go in the grace and peace of the Lord who frees us from our sins.
R. Thanks be to God.

ALBERT CARPENTIER, OP

Services of Reconciliation
Christmas, Two

THEME: THE FAITHFULNESS OF GOD.

Greeting and Introduction

In the name of the Father ...

Grace, mercy and peace be with you from God the Father and Jesus Christ, our Saviour.

The liturgy of Advent is full of calls to 'get ready', to 'wake up', to prepare ourselves for the coming of Christ. We prepare our homes and our streets for Christmas. It would be a pity if we didn't prepare ourselves.

In celebrating the sacrament of reconciliation we are preparing the house of our souls to welcome our Saviour. Let us not be afraid to do some house-cleaning. [Pause]

Opening prayer

God our Father, you loved the world so much that you sent your only Son, not to condemn the world, but to save the world. Cleanse our hearts with your grace, and strengthen our will in doing good, so that your Son may find an eager welcome at his coming. We ask this through the same Christ our Lord.

Scripture Reading: (Luke 1:67-79).

Zechariah was filled with the Holy Spirit and said:
'Blessed be the Lord, the God of Israel,
for he has visited his people, and set them free.
He has raised up for us a mighty saviour in the House of his servant David, just as he had proclaimed by the mouth of his holy prophets from ancient times.
This was the oath he swore to our father Abraham,
that he would grant us, free from fear,
to be delivered from the hands of our enemies,

to serve him in holiness and uprightness all the days of our lives.
And you, little child, will be called the prophet of the Most High,
for you will go before the Lord to prepare a way for him,
to give his people knowledge of salvation through the forgiveness of
their sins.
Because of the faithful love of our God,
the rising Sunhas come from on high to visit us,
to give light to those who live in darkness
and in the shadow of death,
and to guide our feet into the way of peace.'
This is the Gospel of the Lord.

Reflecting on the Scripture Reading

From this reading we see that God is faithful. He is true to his word.
He keeps his promises. All the wanderings, infidelities and sins of his
people are swept aside, and he comes, just as he said he would by
means of his mouthpieces, the prophets.

God comes to us too in spite of our sins and infidelities. He comes,
not as a judge, but as a saviour. He comes to free us from our sins, and
to deliver us from the power of evil. He comes to free us from fear, and
to enable us to live good and holy lives. He comes to give us light when
we walk in darkness and in the shadow of death.

He comes to guide our feet into the way of peace.

It's easier to trust in God at Christmas than at any other time,
because we feel that God is very close to us and very loving towards
us at this time. In Jesus, God comes to us in the form of a child. And
surely no one can be afraid of a child?

Litany of sin (adults)
R. Lord, have mercy.

For not putting you, our Lord and God, first in our lives; for putting
false gods before you. R.

For the irreverent and profane way we have sometimes used your
holy name. R.

For our weak and half-hearted faith. R.

For the routine and thoughtless worship we have sometimes given to you during mass. R.

For the hurt we have done to you in our families, and among our friends and neighbours. R.

For being insensitive to others, using abusive language to them. R.

For sometimes being bad-tempered and hard to live with. R.

For being too ready to find fault. R.

For refusing courtesy and friendship to people we don't like. R.

For refusing to forgive those who have offended us. R.

For regarding ourselves as superior to others, and treating them as inferior. R.

For our broken promises and infidelities. R.

For our lack of honesty in our dealings with others, and our lack of respect for their property. R.

For neglecting the poor, the sick, and those in need. R.

For sometimes endangering ourselves and others through the abuse of alcohol or drugs. R.

For indulging ourselves by using pornographic materials. R.

For the abuse of our sexual powers by ourselves or with others. R.
[Pause]

Litany of sin (teenagers)

R. Lord, have mercy.

For not giving God the place in my life that he should have, and for not praying as often as I should. R.

For the irreverent way I have sometimes used God's name.

For my weak and half-hearted faith. R.

For the times I didn't worship God on Sunday, and for the careless way I have sometimes attended Mass. R.

For the hurt I have caused to others in word or in deed. R.

For refusing to help out at home. R.

For sometimes being bad-tempered and hard to get on with. R.

For the rows and trouble I have caused. R.

For being selfish, and refusing to share with others. R.

For the times a friend needed a hand and I wasn't there when needed. R.

For being too ready to find fault. R.

For refusing to forgive those who have offended me. R.

For the times I was lazy. R.

For the times I was greedy. R.

For the times I was selfish. R.

For the times I have regarded myself as superior to others. R.

For promises I have broken. R.

For the times I have been ungrateful. R.

For taking what didn't belong to me. R.

For endangering myself and through drink or drugs. R.

For not respecting myself. R.

[Pause]

Confiteor

My brothers and sisters, let us call to mind the goodness of God, and acknowledge our sins, so that we may receive his merciful forgiveness.

I confess to almighty God ...

Let us join in the prayer that Jesus taught us, asking God to forgive us as we forgive others.

Our Father ...

(The priests go to the places assigned for confession. The penitents who desire to confess their sins go to the priest of their choice. When the service is celebrated without a priest, participants might reflect on their need for pardon and make an act of contrition.)

Prayers after confession / reflection on the need for pardon

Let us pray that the whole world may be flooded with the grace of the Lord's coming.

R. Come, Lord Jesus.

Come into our hearts. R.

Come into our homes. R.

Come to those who are lonely. R.

Come to those who are fearful. R.

Come to those who are poor. R.

Come to those who are sick. R.

Come to those who are grieving. R.

Come to who are away from home. R.

Come to those who have no faith. R.

Come to those who are without hope. R.

Come to those who are without love. R.

Come to the victims of violence. R.

Come to those in the grip of addiction. R.

Come to those in prison. R.

Come to each of us. R.

Prayer of thanksgiving

God of power and love, we thank you for your goodness to us. Help us to rise above our human weakness, and fill our hearts with your love through the coming of your Son. We ask this through Christ our Lord.

Blessing and Dismissal:

R. Amen.

May the Lord enable you to serve him in holiness and justice all the days of your life.

May the Lord free you from fear and guide your feet into the way of peace.

May the Lord give you light when you walk darkness and in the shadow of death.

Go in the grace and peace of the Lord who frees us from our sins.

R. Thanks be to God.